The Giant Book of Bizarre Facts

By
Jake Jacobs

Kindle Edition

* * * * *

Published by Jake Jacobs at Amazon Kindle

1.

The success of “Bill & Ted's Excellent Adventure” led to the creation of a cereal called "Bill & Ted's Excellent Cereal".

Reference: (https://en.wikipedia.org/wiki/Bill_%26_Ted%27s_Excellent_Cereal)

2.

The actress who played Deborah from “The Office”, who Michael Scott thought was very beautiful, played the Miss Pawnee beauty pageant winner in “Parks and Recreation.”

Reference: (http://theoffice.wikia.com/wiki/Deborah_Shoshlefski)

3.

Finland has a national basketball team that is sponsored by Microsoft.

Reference: (https://en.wikipedia.org/wiki/Finland_national_basketball_team)

4.

Coca-Cola makes a laxative version of Coke in Japan.

Reference: (http://www.coca-colacompany.com/stories/coca-cola-fortified-with-dietary-fiber-to-launch-in-japan)

5.

Niagara Falls is moving upstream at a slowed rate due to human intervention. It was estimated to be moving over a meter per year, which is now down to about 30 centimeters per year.

Reference: (https://www.niagaraparks.com/visit-niagara-parks/plan-your-visit/niagara-falls-geology-facts-figures/)

6.

A con woman, the "Diesel Mystic" of Zimbabwe, convinced Robert Mugabe's cabinet she could tap a rock and produce diesel fuel.

Reference: (http://www.newzimbabwe.com/NEWS-698-Diesel+mystic+faces+jail/NEWS.aspx)

7.

There is a river in California named the "Russian River". It’s 110 miles, or 177 kilometers, long.

Reference: (https://en.wikipedia.org/wiki/Russian_River_(California))

8.

Keanu Reeves actually trained with guns and judo to get ready to play John Wick in "John Wick: Chapter 2".

Reference: (https://www.youtube.com/watch?v=QnB07wnDJL8&feature=youtu.be)

9.

Mount Everest was named after George Everest, whose name is pronounced EVE-REST, not EVER-EST.

Reference: (https://en.wikipedia.org/wiki/George_Everest)

10.

In Norway, everyone's salary is public record, and searchable online.

Reference: (http://www.bbc.co.uk/news/magazine-40669239)

11.

The word "sepia" used to mean "cuttlefish", because that's what color ink it secreted. Before that, it meant "rotten".

Reference: (https://mashedradish.com/2017/10/20/dirty-rotten-sepia/)

12.

Deborah Servitto is a Michigan court of appeals judge who delivered her ruling in the case of DeAngelo Bailey v. Eminem partially in the form of a rap rhyme.

Reference: (https://en.wikipedia.org/wiki/Deborah_Servitto)

13.

Dante Alighieri, author of the Divine Comedy, has never found rest. After dying in Ravenna, he was exhumed on his 600th birthday where an admirer reached into his tomb and grabbed a handful of ashes. It was split into six bags, four of which are still missing to this day.

Reference: (http://news.bbc.co.uk/2/hi/europe/398850.stm)

14.

Ian Fleming's last words were an apology to his ambulance drivers; "I am sorry to trouble you chaps. I don't know how you get along so fast with the traffic on the roads these days".

Reference: (https://en.wikipedia.org/wiki/Ian_Fleming#Death)

15.

Strawberry leaves are good to eat.

Reference: (https://spoonuniversity.com/lifestyle/can-you-eat-strawberry-leaves)

16.

In 1969, Bill Cosby won a Man of the Year award and jokingly suggested re-naming the award, "The nice guy as far as we know", award.

Reference: (https://www.huffingtonpost.com/entry/bill-cosby-damning-joke_us_55bbb82ee4b0b23e3ce2aa5d)

17.

Lucasfilm patented Darth Vader's breathing sound. Sounds being patented are known as "soundmarks".

Reference: (https://gizmodo.com/even-the-sound-of-darth-vader-breathing-is-trademarked-1642863935)

18.

A Buddha statue was found to contain a mummified monk. At the time, such monks believed "self-mummification" was the path to enlightenment and reverence. Monks would starve themselves for a decade, be sealed inside a statue, and subsist on a minimal diet until death.

Reference: (http://blogs.discovermagazine.com/d-brief/2015/02/23/x-rays-buddhist-statue-mummified-monk/#.Wp_1YejwaUk)

19.

The British Royal family is named after Windsor Castle, not the other way around.

Reference: (https://www.telegraph.co.uk/news/uknews/queen-elizabeth-II/11693813/How-German-is-the-Queen.html)

20.

In 2008, during the European Olympic pre-qualifying tournament for ice hockey, Slovakia's women's team beat Bulgaria's 82-0. Slovakia had 139 shots on goal and averaged a point every 44 seconds.

Reference: (http://www.espn.com/olympics/news/story?id=3577150)

21.

WALL-E, the Pixar film, is dedicated to Justin Wright. Justin was 12 when he had a heart transplant and his Make-a-Wish was to visit Pixar. He survived the transplant and later became an animator at Pixar. He died of a massive heart attack 3 months before its release.

Reference: (https://spectrummagazine.org/node/768)

22.

Paul D. Hubbard was a deaf American football player who invented the huddle to communicate without opponents interpreting him.

Reference: (https://en.wikipedia.org/wiki/Paul_D._Hubbard)

23.

J.P. Morgan, of JPMorgan and Chase Co. Banking, and Milton Hershey, of Hershey's Chocolate, were both in Europe and planned to travel back to the United States on Titanic's Maiden Voyage but made other plans.

Reference: (https://www.smithsonianmag.com/history/seven-famous-people-who-missed-the-titanic-101902418/)

24.

Laura Bridgman was the first deaf and blind American child to gain a significant education in the English language, fifty years before the more famous Helen Keller.

Reference: (https://en.wikipedia.org/wiki/Laura_Bridgman)

25.

The Commissariat Department, which was responsible for supplying the British army during the Crimean War, sent them a shipment of boots, with all the left boots on one ship and all the right boots on another. One of the ships sank.

Reference: (http://www.victorianweb.org/history/crimea/blunder2.html)

26.

The Weather Channel released a compilation of the music used during their “Local on the 8s” segment. It peaked #1 on the Billboard Top 100 chart for Contemporary Jazz.

Reference: (https://thump.vice.com/en_us/article/xyp7aq/weather-channel-music-local-on-the-8s-smooth-jazz)

27.

Bruce Lee's son, actor Brandon Lee, died after an accidental shooting on a movie set.

Reference: (https://en.wikipedia.org/wiki/Brandon_Lee#Death)

28.

Weird Al Jankovic only makes a parody if the artist of the original song approves. This policy stems from a misunderstanding that occurred with Amish Paradise. Al was under the impression that Coolio had given his blessing, but itt turned out that he hated the parody. Weird Al adopted his rule because of this.

Reference: (http://weirdal.wikia.com/wiki/Refused_parodies)

29.

In 1977, Argentina flew a pregnant woman to their military base in Antarctica so she could have the first baby to ever be born on the continent. In doing so, the Argentine government believed this would give them an undisputable claim on the land, but the claim is not recognized internationally.

Reference: (https://everipedia.org/wiki/Emilio_Palma/)

30.

The origin of paper planes dates back to 500 BCE, in Ancient China.

Reference: (https://en.wikipedia.org/wiki/Paper_plane)

31.

People who are born deaf and are experiencing voice hallucinations do not "hear" them, but rather see them signed or a mouth forming the word.

Reference: (http://www.ucl.ac.uk/news/news-articles/0707/07070303)

32.

The pterodactyl is not actually a dinosaur, but a pterosaur which were airborne reptiles of the Late Jurassic period.

Reference: (http://dinosaurpictures.org/Pterodactyl-pictures)

33.

Australia once had a tumbleweed so large they named it "Hairy Panic".

Reference: (https://www.theguardian.com/australia-news/2016/feb/18/fast-growing-tumbleweed-called-hairy-panic-blows-into-australian-city)

34.

The 1990 England World Cup song, “World in Motion” by New Order, was originally called “E for England”, but was vetoed by the FA, because of the rampant ecstasy drug culture in England at the time.

Reference: (http://www.nme.com/blogs/nme-blogs/world-in-motion-25-years-on-10-geeky-facts-about-the-new-order-football-classic-7523)

35.

The oldest D20 dice was uncovered in Egypt and dates back around 30 BC.

Reference: (https://www.cnet.com/news/ancient-d20-die-emerges-from-the-ashes-of-time/)

36.

Hair is made of dead cells.

Reference: (https://kidshealth.org/en/kids/hair.html)

37.

The compilation album “Legend” by Bob Marley and the Wailers has charted in the Billboard 200 for 992 nonconsecutive weeks. The only album to succeed this is Pink Floyd's “Dark Side of the Moon”.

Reference: (https://en.wikipedia.org/wiki/Legend_(Bob_Marley_and_the_Wailers_album))

38.

Indonesia is made up of over 16,000 islands and the Indonesian government has managed to name each island.

Reference: (http://www.ppk-kp3k.kkp.go.id/direktori-pulau/index.php/public_c/pulau_data)

39.

Wilkes Land crater underneath the ice in Antarctica is the most probable cause of the Permian Extinction Event.

Reference: (https://www.space.com/2452-giant-crater-tied-worst-mass-extinction.html)

40.

On request of the family of Sir Winston Churchill, there is always a marmalade cat called Jock in residence at Chartwell House. Currently it is Jock VI.

Reference: (https://www.nationaltrust.org.uk/chartwell/features/jock-vi-of-chartwell)

41.

There's an IMAX theatre at the South Rim of the Grand Canyon that has only one showing: a 35 minute film highlighting the history and the beauty of the canyon.

Reference: (https://explorethecanyon.com/imax-theater/)

42.

Steve Comisar is a man who sold "solar powered clothes dryers" for $49.95 in national magazines. Unsuspecting customers would receive a length of clothes line.

Reference: (http://www.shenhuifu.org/2017/07/07/most-clever-scams/?relatedpic)

43.

Abraham Lincoln, prior to becoming President, was an avid boater and traveled on the Ohio and Mississippi rivers where his boat often got stuck on sandbars. In 1849, Lincoln invented a method for buoying vessels over shoals, making him the first and only U.S. President to receive a patent.

Reference: (https://en.wikipedia.org/wiki/Abraham_Lincoln%27s_patent)

44.

An average American adult spends 93% of their life indoors.

Reference: (https://snowbrains.com/brain-post-much-time-average-american-spend-outdoors/)

45.

Alaskan killer whales have been documented hunting and eating swimming moose.

Reference: (http://environmentalaska.us/orcas.html)

46.

Hampshire College has a visiting non-human scholar, Physarum Policephalum, a plasmodial slime mold.

Reference: (https://www.hampshire.edu/faculty/physarum-polycephalum)

47.

Slash's mother was a costume designer for David Bowie among others; his father created album covers for Joni Mitchell and Neil Young.

Reference: (https://en.wikipedia.org/wiki/Slash_%28musician%29)

48.

The ship upon whose mutiny the book "The Hunt for Red October" was based was not trying to defect to the west, but was in fact trying to spark a second communist revolution.

Reference: (http://www.executedtoday.com/2010/08/03/1976-valery-sablin-hunt-for-red-october-inspiration/)

49.

The last book that Indian Freedom Fighter Bhagat Singh was reading before he hanged was a biography of the Russian leader Lenin.

Reference: (https://www.hindustantimes.com/india/bhagat-singh-the-final-hours/story-oHHsDEhtugs4wSI7dfWuzO.html)

50.

In 2014, Singapore's anti-gambling agency, in a bid to leverage the World Cup fever, published an advert that showed a worried kid telling his friend that his father had bet all their savings on Germany winning the World Cup. Germany won.

Reference: (http://www.bbc.com/news/world-asia-28318187)

51.

The word "paradise" entered the English language from the French "paradis," inherited from the Latin "paradisus," from Greek "parádeisos," from an Old Iranian word "paridayda," meaning "walled enclosure".

Reference: (https://en.wikipedia.org/wiki/Paradise)

52.

1 meter was originally defined as one ten-millionth of the distance between the equator and the North Pole through Paris.

Reference: (https://physics.nist.gov/cuu/Units/meter.html)

53.

The Japanese pilot who attacked a town in Oregon during World War II returned years later to present his family's 400-year-old samurai sword to the city as a symbol of regret.

Reference: (https://www.sharpen-up.com/japanese-ww2-pilot-presents-familys-400-year-old-sword-u-s-town-symbol-regret/)

54.

Robin Williams' will prevents Disney from using his name, taped performances or voice recordings until 2039, after which they will be able to create Aladdin 2 using his real voice.

Reference: (http://www.huffingtonpost.ca/entry/aladdin-sequel-robin-williams-will_us_564244fee4b0411d3072cda4)

55.

The collective term for a group of butterflies is a kaleidoscope.

Reference: (https://en.wikipedia.org/wiki/List_of_English_terms_of_venery,_by_animal#B)

56.

In 1838, General Antonio López de Santa Anna had his leg amputated after his ankle was destroyed by canon-fire. He ordered a full military burial for it.

Reference: (http://historythings.com/time-santa-anna-held-funeral-amputated-leg/)

57.

Giraffes and their milk are kosher.

Reference: (https://en.wikipedia.org/wiki/Kashrut#Permitted_and_forbidden_animals)

58.

During Operation Rolling Thunder, a massive bombing campaign on North Vietnam which killed 180,000 civilians, the U.S. dropped more bombs in 3 years than it used during the entire Pacific Theater of World War II.

Reference: (https://en.wikipedia.org/wiki/Operation_Rolling_Thunder)

59.

A Canadian man was assaulted with bacon and eggs.

Reference: (http://www.cbc.ca/news/canada/hamilton/news/bacon-and-eggs-assault-teen-uses-breakfast-as-weapon-police-1.3460252)

60.

A newly discovered carnivorous jungle plant, Nepenthes Attenboroughii, gobbles up rats whole.

Reference: (https://www.popsci.com/environment/article/2009-08/newly-discovered-plant-species-eats-rats-named-after-famous-naturalist)

61.

The album cover for Nirvana's "Nevermind" was inspired after Kurt Cobain watched a documentary on water births. After the record label denied them to use a picture of a water birth, they went to a pool with photographer Kirk Weddle, who captured a shot of his friend's son swimming.

Reference: (https://www.rollingstone.com/music/lists/nirvanas-nevermind-10-things-you-didnt-know-w441220)

62.

Paralympic medals make different sounds to differentiate gold, silver, and bronze.

Reference: (https://youtu.be/LWRj67Lp7Z4?t=312)

63.

After the Romanian Revolution in 1989, many orphanages were shut down forcing thousands of neglected orphans to live in the sewers of Bucharest. Many of those orphans still live in the sewers today, some have even raised their children there.

Reference: (http://abcnews.go.com/International/life-tunnels-inside-underground-world-bucharest-romanias-sewer/story?id=27200275)

64.

In 1966, there was a sharp decrease in the Japanese birthrate because it was considered unlucky for a woman to be born that year, so many families aborted their female babies.

Reference: (http://www.randalolson.com/2016/05/08/why-did-so-many-japanese-families-avoid-having-children-in-1966/)

65.

The Quran says that Jesus did not die on the cross, but it was made to appear that way.

Reference: (https://en.wikipedia.org/wiki/Islamic_views_on_Jesus%27_death)

66.

The name for the shape a classic soccer ball is based on is called a "truncated icosahedron".

Reference: (https://www.youtube.com/watch?v=cwWBpjeyRS0)

67.

In the early 19th century, the Scottish soldier Gregor MacGregor tricked hundreds of people into investing in and emigrating to a fictional Central American territory called "Poyais."

Reference: (https://en.wikipedia.org/wiki/Gregor_MacGregor)

68.

Dr. Seuss's Whoville is as small as a speck of dust on a clover, meaning that the Grinch is too.

Reference: (https://en.wikipedia.org/wiki/Whoville)

69.

A war was once fought in Canada over the trade of pemmican, a concentrated mixture of fat and protein used as a nutritious food, usually made from bison.

Reference: (https://en.wikipedia.org/wiki/Pemmican_War)

70.

In World War I, the military would use a camouflage called “dazzle camouflage” to make it harder for the enemy to estimate the range, speed and heading of a ship, henceforth making it harder to successfully sink the ship.

Reference: (https://publicdomainreview.org/collections/dazzle-ships/)

71.

The U.S. government once attempted to use New Age philosophy and harness the powers of the paranormal for military operations. Rumor has it that one soldier was able to kill a goat by staring at it.

Reference: (https://en.wikipedia.org/wiki/The_Men_Who_Stare_at_Goats)

72.

In 1992, Singapore introduced a ban on normal, not medical or dental chewing gum, because vandals used it to interrupt the doors on their trains.

Reference: (http://www.bbc.com/news/magazine-32090420)

73.

Future president John Adams wanted us to call the president "his majesty."

Reference:(https://www.senate.gov/artandhistory/history/minute/John_Adams_Senate_Farewell.htm)

74.

The word "dinosaur" comes from Ancient Greek meaning "terrible lizard".

Reference: (https://en.wikipedia.org/wiki/Dinosaur#Etymology)

75.

Winnie the Pooh's first name is Edward.

Reference: (https://en.wikipedia.org/wiki/When_We_Were_Very_Young)

76.

Nicotine may actually have an upside by replacing missing neurotransmitters, and functioning in the prevention and treatment of Parkinson's disease. However, the benefits don't outweigh the risks, say medical doctors.

Reference: (https://www.nytimes.com/2016/03/06/opinion/sunday/can-nicotine-be-good-for-you.html)

77.

In May 1997, a Japanese student was beheaded and further mutilated before being left in front of an elementary school with a note in similar style to the American Zodiac Killings. A 14-year-old boy was arrested and confessed to a similar murder that occurred in March.

Reference: (https://en.wikipedia.org/wiki/Kobe_child_murders)

78.

Ukrainian authorities told Pripyat citizens to drink vodka to help with radiation shortly after Chernobyl disaster.

Reference: (https://www.eurozine.com/the-vodka-was-supposed-to-cleanse-our-thyroid-glands/)

79.

The term "the best and the brightest" originally came from a title of a book about the origins of the Vietnam War and was supposed to be highly ironic and satirical.

Reference: (https://en.wikipedia.org/wiki/The_Best_and_the_Brightest)

80.

Abolitionists used maple syrup in their cooking because molasses and cane sugar were both slave crops.

Reference: (https://en.wikipedia.org/wiki/Maple_syrup)

81.

Von Miller majored in Poultry Sciences and runs his own chicken farm.

Reference: (https://en.wikipedia.org/wiki/Von_Miller)

82.

Ed McMahon, Johnny Carson's sidekick, was a carrier certified Marine F4U Corsair instructor pilot during World War II and an artillery spotter during the Korean War. He flew a total of 85 combat missions. After the war, he stayed with the Marines as a reserve officer, retiring in 1966 as a colonel.

Reference: (https://www.wikipedia.org/wiki/Ed_McMahon)

83.

Ernestine Shepherd began bodybuilding at 56 years old and was declared the oldest female competitive bodybuilder at age 75. She is still going strong today at the age of 81, having won several competitions and marathons.

Reference: (https://en.wikipedia.org/wiki/Ernestine_Shepherd)

84.

Rudolf Höss' right-hand man, Robert Mulka, was located and subsequently arrested for war crimes after World War II because an attorney from the Frankfurt Public Prosecutor's read about Mulka's son winning a Bronze Medal for Yachting in the 1960 Rome Olympics.

Reference: (https://en.wikipedia.org/wiki/Robert_Mulka)

85.

The reason almost no nation has purple on their flag is because purple dye was prohibitively expensive up until the late 19th century.

Reference: (https://www.youtube.com/watch?v=CYB-pmNs4VQ)

86.

The Japanese-style strike, "Huelga a la japonesa", is a Spanish urban legend about union pressure in which the workers would work harder in order to generate overproduction and create economic disruption.

Reference: (https://en.wikipedia.org/wiki/Huelga_a_la_japonesa)

87.

Cavemen had tattoos. Ötzi the Iceman from 3250 B.C. had 61 tattoos across his body.

Reference: (https://insider.si.edu/2015/12/debate-over-worlds-oldest-tattoo-is-over-for-now/)

88.

The Black Death that wiped out half of Europe's population in the Middle Ages was spread by humans, not rats.

Reference: (http://www.pnas.org/content/early/2018/01/09/1715640115)

89.

Chicago Cubs player Rick Monday was in the outfield when he saw two protestors run onto the grass trying to burn an American flag. Before they did, Monday took it from them to an ovation from the crowd. When he went to bat later, the message board read "RICK MONDAY... YOU MADE A GREAT PLAY..."

Reference: (https://en.wikipedia.org/wiki/Rick_Monday#American_flag_incident)

90.

In a room with 23 people, it's more likely than unlikely that at least two of them share the same birthday.

Reference: (https://betterexplained.com/articles/understanding-the-birthday-paradox/)

91.

The second-most murderous serial killer of modern history has his whereabouts currently unknown ever since being released from prison 20 years ago.

Reference: (https://en.wikipedia.org/wiki/Pedro_L%C3%B3pez_(serial_killer))

92.

The Garbage Pail Kids were made into a live action movie in 1987, with a cast of little people.

Reference: (https://www.flickeringmyth.com/2017/08/30-years-of-trash-the-true-story-behind-the-garbage-pail-kids-movie/)

93.

The two parts to the word “helicopter” are not “heli” and “copter”, but “helico” meaning spiral, and “pter” meaning one with wings, like pterodactyl.

Reference: (https://en.wikipedia.org/wiki/Helicopter)

94.

Saltwater Brewery introduced edible six-pack rings to help alleviate the issue with how they injured sea animals, most notably turtles and seabirds.

Reference: (https://www.smithsonianmag.com/smart-news/brewery-introduces-edible-biodegrable-six-pack-rings-180959172/)

95.

A Wyoming woman maintains and regularly uses a 122 year old sourdough starter to make pancakes. The starter is older than the state of Wyoming itself.

Reference: (http://trib.com/news/state-and-regional/newcastle-woman-maintains--year-old-sourdough-starter/article_000fcb17-5a5a-5590-84c2-3b55bb1d80fa.html)

96.

Ann Wilson of Heart wrote the song Barracuda after her recording company created a rumor that her sister and her were having an incestuous relationship for publicity. Following a concert, a fan asked how her “lover” was. Enraged, she went directly to her hotel room and began writing the lyrics.

Reference: (https://en.wikipedia.org/wiki/Barracuda_(song))

97.

The South Korean executive office is called the "Blue House".

Reference: (https://en.wikipedia.org/wiki/Blue_House)

98.

Machetes in English-Speaking Caribbean countries are referred to as a "Cutlass".

Reference: (https://en.wikipedia.org/wiki/Cutlass#Etymology)

99.

Germany has a different name depending on which peoples you ask. Scandinavians call it Tyskland, Poles call it Niemcy, Portuguese call it Alemanha, Italians call it Germania, French call it Allemagne, the Dutch call it Duitsland, and even the Germans themselves call it Deutschland.

Reference: (https://www.oktoberfesthaus.com/blogs/okt/161688647-why-do-we-call-deutschland-germany)

100.

Razorback pigs are an invasive species in the United States and are descended from domesticated pigs that escaped from one of the first Spanish explorations of North America in the 1500s.

Reference:(https://en.wikipedia.org/wiki/Hernando_de_Soto#Effects_of_expedition_in_North_America)

101.

Navy Seal Mike Day was shot 27 times and still defeated the enemy. Currently, he does triathlons to benefit wounded veteran programs.

Reference: (https://taskandpurpose.com/unsung-heroes-this-navy-seal-kept-fighting-after-getting-shot-27-times/)

102.

There is an island in Massachusetts named after the rapper Busta Rhymes.

Reference: (https://en.wikipedia.org/wiki/Busta_Rhymes_Island)

103.

Just 6% of the U.K. is built on, the rest is free land.

Reference: (https://www.sheffield.ac.uk/news/nr/land-cover-atlas-uk-1.744440)

104.

Werner Herzog, the documentary filmmaker, once ate his shoe because he lost a bet. He made a documentary out of it.

Reference: (https://en.wikipedia.org/wiki/Werner_Herzog_Eats_His_Shoe)

105.

When Candid Camera host Allen Funt's airplane was hijacked by Cubans, the passengers believed they were on a hidden camera television show. He could not change their minds.

Reference: (https://uproxx.com/tv/the-time-a-real-plane-hijacking-was-mistaken-for-a-candid-camera-stunt/)

106.

Wheelchair Boxing is a sport that aims to be a part of the Paralympics.

Reference: (http://www.bbc.com/sport/get-inspired/35911497)

107.

Since 1971, there have only been 15 Oscar Ceremony's when composer John Williams wasn't nominated for an Academy Award. However, he has only won one since 1982.

Reference: (https://en.wikipedia.org/wiki/John_Williams#Academy_Awards)

108.

There was once a breed of dog called the Turnspit dog which would run in a wheel to turn meat so it would cook evenly. The breed went extinct when machines were invented to turn the meat instead.

Reference: (https://en.wikipedia.org/wiki/Turnspit_dog)

109.

One of Karl Heinz Stockhausen's best known compositions includes four helicopters.

Reference: (https://en.wikipedia.org/wiki/Helikopter-Streichquartett)

110.

"Trepanning" is a process by which an individual has holes drilled into their skull. The practice goes back for thousands of years and while it's a genuine medical practice to relieve brain swelling or bleeding, people have begun doing it for pseudoscientific and spiritual purposes.

Reference: (https://en.wikipedia.org/wiki/Trepanning)

111.

To ensure Kendrick Lamar didn't have a "ghostwriter", Eminem kicked everyone out of the studio and made Kendrick write an entire verse on the spot.

Reference: (https://massappeal.com/that-one-time-eminem-made-sure-kendrick-lamar-didnt-have-a-ghostwriter/)

112.

Vasco de Quiroga, is a Mexican bishop who established small quasi-socialist communities based on Thomas More's book “Utopia”, which is where the word comes from. He is venerated as a saint by some to the modern day.

Reference: (https://en.wikipedia.org/wiki/Vasco_de_Quiroga)

113.

In 1998, in the Democratic Republic of Congo, lightning struck in the field during a football match. 11 people died, all of the same team. The players from the other team were left unharmed. The whole thing even led to accusations of cursing and witchcraft.

Reference: (http://www.independent.co.uk/news/lightning-kills-an-entire-football-team-1181336.html)

114.

Scott Tucker is estimated to have earned $380 million from his payday loan organization, which exploited Native American sovereign immunity laws to offer predatory payday loans in states in which they are illegal.

Reference: (https://en.wikipedia.org/wiki/Scott_Tucker_(racing_driver))

115.

A patriotic song in Luxembourg, infamous European tax paradise, already had the line, "no taxes will crush us", in 1859.

Reference: (https://lb.wikipedia.org/wiki/De_Feierwon)

116.

The leaders of the infamous human experimentation, including vivisection of pregnant women, and amputation without anesthesia, in Unit 731 were secretly granted full immunity in exchange for sharing their test results with the U.S.

Reference: (https://en.wikipedia.org/wiki/Unit_731#American_grant_of_immunity)

117.

Hugh Jackman buys lottery tickets for the entire cast and crew every Friday while filming a movie. It's a tradition he started in an effort to get to know one another and encourage comradery and team work among the crew.

Reference: (https://www.youtube.com/watch?v=8LNOPDjlYmA&t=6m33s)

118.

The ingredients that are used to make Flamin' Hot Cheetos spicy are not made publicly available. None of the ingredients listed on the packaging are actually hot.

Reference: (https://www.wired.com/2016/04/whats-inside-flamin-hot-cheetos/)

119.

Whitney Houston's cover of "I Will Always Love You" is a recording of the first time she ever sang it.

Reference: (http://ew.com/article/2012/12/14/oral-history-whitneys-anthem-i-will-always-love-you/)

120.

During an 11-year period, from about 1964 to 1975, the office of the Vice President of the United States was vacant for a total of 617 days.

Reference: (https://en.wikipedia.org/wiki/List_of_Presidents_of_the_United_States)

121.

Having a store credit card can raise your auto insurance premiums.

Reference: (https://personalreports.lexisnexis.com/lexisnexis_attract_auto_score/sample.jsp)

122.

There are many hybrid animals and some with names like Zeedonk, which is a zebra and donkey mix, Wholphin, which is a whale and dolphin mix, and Cama, which is a camel and lama mix.

Reference: (https://en.wikipedia.org/wiki/List_of_genetic_hybrids)

123.

In the 1950s, it was fashionable for men who wore shorts to wear knee high socks, often in colorful argyle styles. Between the long Bermuda shorts and the knee high socks, usually only the knee remained uncovered.

Reference: (https://vintagedancer.com/1950s/mens-1950s-clothing-history-casual/)

124.

After the murder of civil rights activist Medgar Evers in 1963, his alleged murderer was tried by an all-white jury who deadlocked twice and failed to convict. In 1994, Evers was discovered to be so well embalmed that forensic autopsy was still possible, leading to his murderer's conviction.

Reference: (https://en.wikipedia.org/wiki/Embalming#Notable_embalmings)

125.

Matt Bellamy's father was a guitarist in "The Tornados", which was the 1st British band with an American #1 hit "Telstar".

Reference: (https://en.wikipedia.org/wiki/Matt_Bellamy)

126.

There's a traditional dish in Northern Brazil that involves boiling Manioc leaves for a week to remove its high content of cyanide.

Reference: (https://en.wikipedia.org/wiki/Mani%C3%A7oba)

127.

The federal government spent about $350 billion during World War II, or twice as much as it had spent in total for the entire history of the U.S. government up to that point.

Reference: (http://www.dummies.com/education/history/american-history/u-s-economy-and-industry-during-world-war-ii/)

128.

In 2001, Belgium planned to replace soda with beer in school children's lunches.

Reference: (https://www.theguardian.com/world/2001/jun/21/schools.education)

129.

The U.S. Navy fought a battle against the Japanese during the Civil War.

Reference: (https://en.wikipedia.org/wiki/Battle_of_Shimonoseki_Straits)

130.

Augustus Cole from the Gears of War video game was voiced by Terry Tate, office linebacker.

Reference: (https://en.wikipedia.org/wiki/Lester_Speight)

131.

There are over 650 species of entirely freshwater crabs.

Reference: (https://en.wikipedia.org/wiki/Potamidae)

132.

Air travel was practically unaffected on January 1st, 2000, even though mass panic about the Y2K bug was at its height.

Reference: (https://www.deseretnews.com/article/807380/Airline-travel-appears-unaffected-by-Y2K-bug.html)

133.

The original M-80 was used by the U. S. military to simulate explosions and used 3,000 milligrams of powder, but are illegal without a federal license. The legal ones sold as fireworks only have 50 milligrams of powder, or 1/60th as much as the military version.

Reference: (https://en.wikipedia.org/wiki/M-80_(explosive))

134.

The skin of a honey badger is tough enough to resist several machete blows and is almost impervious to arrows and spears.

Reference: (https://en.wikipedia.org/wiki/Honey_badger#Relationships_with_humans)

135.

People used to think sparrows hibernate at the bottom of lakes during the winter.

Reference: (https://www.uh.edu/engines/epi2228.htm)

136.

The famous French playwright Molière was buried in the part of the cemetery reserved for unbaptized infants, as actors were not allowed to be buried in the sacred ground of a cemetery. .

Reference: (https://en.wikipedia.org/wiki/Moli%C3%A8re#Death)

137.

During the Great Chinese Famine between 1959 and 1961, drought, poor weather, and the policies of ruler Mao Zedong caused an estimated tens of millions of deaths due to starvation.

Reference: (https://en.wikipedia.org/wiki/Great_Chinese_Famine)

138.

The "big fat phony" guy from Family Guy is credited as "Holden Caulfield", who is the protagonist of Catcher in the Rye who often accuses people of being "phony".

Reference: (http://familyguy.wikia.com/wiki/Holden_Caulfield)

139.

For 13 days, The Beatles had a new drummer after Ringo Starr was hospitalized. He even wore Ringo's suits, but the trousers were far too short.

Reference: (https://www.thescottishsun.co.uk/living/266605/the-sad-story-of-jimmie-nicol-who-became-a-beatle-for-two-weeks-after-standing-in-for-ringo-starr/)

140.

Akinetopsia is a neuropsychological disorder that makes it so patients are unable to perceive motion. Instead, they often view life as a series of photographs or frozen movie reels.

Reference: (https://en.wikipedia.org/wiki/Akinetopsia)

141.

Allen Iverson's mother believes he was conceived without intercourse.

Reference: (https://www.si.com/nba/2015/05/15/allen-iverson-mvp-larry-brown-2001-philadelphia-76ers-vault)

142.

The reason British people say "mum's the word" is because "mum" is a slang version of the 14th century word "momme" which means "be silent" or "do not reveal".

Reference: (https://en.wikipedia.org/wiki/Mum%27s_the_word)

143.

Baby carrots are not naturally mini-sized carrots but they are just cut down to size from imperfect, normal sized carrots.

Reference: (https://www.huffingtonpost.com/entry/baby-carrots-are-liars_us_570d98cce4b03d8b7b9ec7f4)

144.

The bubblegum pop song "Sugar, Sugar" topped Billboard magazine in 1969, beating out legends like the Beatles, Elvis Presley, Marvin Gaye, Stevie Wonder, the Temptations, and the Rolling Stones.

Reference: (https://en.wikipedia.org/wiki/Billboard_Year-End_Hot_100_singles_of_1969)

145.

Kiyoshi Kimura is a sushi restaurant chain CEO who helped reduce Somali pirates activity by giving them training in fisheries, initially sourcing them fishing vessels and networking them to the fishery distribution network, ultimately helping them to become fishermen.

Reference: (https://grapee.jp/en/54127)

146.

Columbus used packs of Spanish war dogs to attack native Indians.

Reference: (http://www.easypetmd.com/doginfo/alano-espanol)

147.

18th century scientists believed that sperm contained tiny preformed humans that implanted in the woman's reproductive system to grow in size.

Reference: (https://en.wikipedia.org/wiki/Preformationism)

148.

NASA's jet powered aircraft, X-43A managed to reach speeds of Mach 9.6.

Reference: (https://www.nasa.gov/missions/research/x43-main.html)

149.

Père Lachaise cemetery in France was so desperate for business that in 1804 the administrators devised a marketing strategy to transfer Jean de La Fontaine and Molière's remains to their cemetery. Soon, people were clamoring to be buried among famous people and their business quadrupled.

Reference: (https://en.wikipedia.org/wiki/P%C3%A8re_Lachaise_Cemetery)

150.

Up to the early 16th century, medical diagnostics was limited to uroscopy, in which doctors used their five senses to examine a patient's urine.

Reference: (https://io9.gizmodo.com/5953234/urine-flavor-wheels-helped-doctors-diagnose-patients-pee-centuries-ago)

151.

Multiple studies have shown that high top sneakers are no more effective than low top sneakers in preventing ankle sprains.

Reference: (http://journals.sagepub.com/doi/abs/10.1177/036354659302100416)

152.

In Māori mythology, Māui tried to bring immortality to humanity, but was killed in the attempt by the goddess of death's obsidian vagina teeth.

Reference: (https://en.wikipedia.org/wiki/M%C4%81ui_(M%C4%81ori_mythology))

153.

Famed studio bass player Carol Kaye offers lessons via Skype.

Reference: (https://www.carolkaye.com/)

154.

There was a Polish doctor named Eugene Lazowski who saved thousands of Jews during the Holocaust by creating a fake epidemic which played on German phobias about hygiene.

Reference: (https://www.revolvy.com/main/index.php?s=Eugene+Lazowski&item_type=topic)

155.

Since 1804, Haiti has had 28 coup d'états or coup attempts. The only country with more is Spain, with a total of 36. Spain's first coup attempt happened in 603, over a thousand years before Haitian independence.

Reference:(https://en.wikipedia.org/wiki/List_of_coups_d%27%C3%A9tat_and_coup_attempts_by_country)

156.

Before Nirvana covered "Where Did You Sleep Last Night", Kurt Cobain provided backing vocals and Krist Novoselic provided bass for Mark Lanegan's rendition of the song on the album The Winding Trees.

Reference: (https://en.wikipedia.org/wiki/The_Winding_Sheet)

157.

Since Elizabeth Short's murder, over 500 people have confessed to being the killer. Her death remains unsolved.

Reference: (https://en.wikipedia.org/wiki/Black_Dahlia#Suspects_and_confessions)

158.

There are 915,103,765 ways to combine six 2x4 Lego bricks of the same color.

Reference: (http://www.bbc.com/news/business-43298897)

159.

Chicago O' Hare airport has the ORD short code because it was originally called Orchard Field and no one bothered to change it when it was renamed.

Reference: (https://en.wikipedia.org/wiki/O%27Hare_International_Airport#History)

160.

The Punisher once made an appearance in the Archie Comics.

Reference: (https://en.wikipedia.org/wiki/Archie_Meets_the_Punisher)

161.

In 1960, three Finnish teenagers were brutally murdered while camping in Lake Bodom. The identity of their killer remains unknown.

Reference: (https://www.youtube.com/watch?v=AAUo9OSbYj4)

162.

License plates in the Northwest Territories, Canada's most northern region, are made in the shape of polar bears.

Reference: (https://www.autotrader.com/car-news/the-license-plate-of-canadas-northwest-territories-is-shaped-like-a-polar-bear-261041)

163.

There was a study where men and women asked people on campus whether they would like to sleep with them. The women had a 75% success rate, the men had 0%.

Reference: (http://www2.hawaii.edu/~elaineh/79.pdf)

164.

Early pacemakers required the user to be constantly plugged in to a wall outlet.

Reference: (https://www.ncbi.nlm.nih.gov/pmc/articles/PMC3232561/)

165.

A small U.S. National Monument is in Waco, Texas to protect the remains of Columbian Mammoths.

Reference: (https://www.cbsnews.com/news/obama-to-create-new-national-monuments-in-texas-california-nevada/)

166.

Jackie Chan voiced Captain Li Shang in the Chinese dub of Mulan and even sang, "I'll Make a Man Out of You."

Reference: (https://en.wikipedia.org/wiki/Mulan_(1998_film))

167.

Sea otters have the densest hair in the world, ranging from about 26,000 to 165,000 hairs per square centimeter.

Reference: (https://seaworld.org/animal-info/animal-infobooks/otters/physical-characteristics)

168.

Giant pandas can have sex over 50 times in a few hours.

Reference: (http://www.bbc.co.uk/earth/story/20150310-the-truth-about-giant-pandas)

169.

Herring communicate by a method known as Fast Repetitive Tick, or FRT.

Reference: (https://news.nationalgeographic.com/news/2003/11/1110_031110_herringfarts.html)

170.

"Twenty One Pilots" band name is taken from a play called "All My Sons" by Arthur Miller.

Reference: (https://en.wikipedia.org/wiki/Twenty_One_Pilots)

171.

There is a monument to laboratory mice at a university in Siberia. The mouse is wearing a lab coat and knitting a DNA double helix, symbolizing the gradual progress of DNA research.

Reference: (https://www.atlasobscura.com/places/monument-to-the-laboratory-mouse)

172.

The Lighthouse of Maracaibo is an atmospheric phenomenon in an Venezuelan lake where lightning strikes 260 nights a year, 10 hours per day and up to 280 times per hour.

Reference: (https://en.wikipedia.org/wiki/Catatumbo_lightning)

173.

The anus is the first thing to form in the womb.

Reference: (https://en.wikipedia.org/wiki/Embryological_origins_of_the_mouth_and_anus)

174.

During World War II, the U.S. government urged Americans to save excess fat rendered from cooking and donate it to the army to produce explosives.

Reference: (https://www.theatlantic.com/health/archive/2014/04/reluctantly-turning-bacon-into-bombs-during-world-war-ii/360298/)

175.

The Ohio Constitution doesn't provide a specific minimum age requirement in order to run for its General Assembly.

Reference: (https://www.sos.state.oh.us/globalassets/publications/election/2018_crg_07.pdf)

176.

In May 2015, a woman unknowingly almost disposed of her husband's Apple I computer and never came forward to collect the money from the auction of it.

Reference: (https://en.wikipedia.org/wiki/Apple_I#cite_note-Cbs2015-05-30-36)

177.

The shortest player in the NBA was Tyrone "Muggsy" Bogues. Muggsy stood at 5'3" and played for a total of 14 seasons.

Reference: (https://www.theplayerstribune.com/muggsy-bogues-nickname/)

178.

There is an alarming number of doctors dying by suicide. In 2012, Dr. Pamela Wible, MD started counting dead doctors. She began with a list of 10. Today she has 699.

Reference: (https://www.kevinmd.com/blog/2018/01/surgeon-suicide-homicide-happened-dr-chris-dawson.html)

179.

In 1944, Franklin Roosevelt was gifted a letter opener made out of the arm bone of a Japanese soldier but had to return it due to the shock and outrage it caused in Japan and the U.S.

Reference:(https://en.wikipedia.org/wiki/American_mutilation_of_Japanese_war_dead#U.S._reaction)

180.

The island nation Kiribati is pronounced "Kiribas".

Reference: (https://en.wikipedia.org/wiki/Kiribati#Etymology)

181.

In the half-century between April, 1964, and April, 2013, only one issue of Mad Magazine was published which didn't contain new material by cartoonist Al Jaffee.

Reference: (https://en.wikipedia.org/wiki/Al_Jaffee)

182.

Princess Alice, Duchess of Gloucester, aunt by marriage to Queen Elizabeth II, was 102 when she died, making her the oldest member of the British royal family in history.

Reference: (https://www.telegraph.co.uk/news/obituaries/1475521/Princess-Alice-Duchess-of-Gloucester.html)

183.

Chinese Crispy Seaweed is actually just cabbage and not seaweed at all.

Reference: (https://en.wikipedia.org/wiki/Edible_seaweed)

184.

Max Martin is a Swedish songwriter and producer who has played a role in 21 number 1 hits in the Billboard Hot 100. Only Paul McCartney, with 32 number 1 hits, and John Lennon with 26 have more.

Reference: (https://www.billboard.com/articles/columns/chart-beat/6664085/ask-billboard-max-martin-has-written-how-many-hot-100-top-10s)

185.

Beethoven composed the famous "Ninth Symphony" after he had gone totally deaf.

Reference: (https://www.dsokids.com/listen/by-composer/ludwig-van-beethoven.aspx)

186.

An endangered parrot in New Zealand would only mate with people's heads, so they made an ejaculation helmet for people to wear. The parrot would have sex with the helmet and the researchers would collect the rare semen.

Reference: (https://www.smithsonianmag.com/science-nature/seduced-rare-parrot-180962855/)

187.

Stalin was a cinephile and all of his homes had a private theater. He took a direct role in helping produce, direct, and write nearly every film released by the Soviet Union under his reign, favoring stories of strong Russians. His favorite films to screen starred Charlie Chaplin and John Wayne.

Reference: (https://www.telegraph.co.uk/culture/3618310/Why-Stalin-loved-Tarzan-and-wanted-John-Wayne-shot.html)

188.

The Doughnut Dollies were women who volunteered with the Red Cross during World War I, World War II and the Vietnam War. They drove Clubmobiles to both bases and field operations to serve soldiers coffee and doughnuts, play hit records and boost morale.

Reference: (http://www.clubmobile.org/history.html)

189.

FalconSAT-2, the payload for one of the first SpaceX Falcon1 launches, fell off of the failed rocket 33 seconds into launch and landed a few feet from the storage container it came in on Omelek Island.

Reference: (https://en.wikipedia.org/wiki/FalconSAT-2)

190.

The sanitary pad belt industry collapsed after the invention of the self-adhesive sanitary pad in the early 1970s. Prior to this, a variety of methods were employed to hold pads in place, including special belts, suspenders and complicated underpants.

Reference: (http://www.mum.org/staynet72.htm)

191.

When Sir Edmund Hillary first conquered Mount Everest he took a pee on the summit before heading back down.

Reference: (https://www.youtube.com/watch?v=SKGwju907KQ)

192.

A piece of the first satellite in space, the Russian Sputnik, landed in Manitowoc, Wisconsin upon reentry and the townspeople created a festival in its honor.

Reference: (https://www.space.com/23029-sputnikfest-soviet-satellite-fall-wisconsin.html)

193.

Rotationplasty is a surgical procedure for young patients that need their lower limb amputated. The section that needs to be amputated is cut out and the foot is reattached backwards, allowing the ankle to function as a replacement knee joint with the prosthetic.

Reference: (http://www.medicaldaily.com/rotationplasty-may-look-strange-some-young-bone-cancer-patients-benefits-are-385072)

194.

Deaf people with Tourette syndrome may involuntarily sign swear words.

Reference: (https://en.wikipedia.org/wiki/Coprolalia)

195.

"The Lost Generation" is a sad poem about society that ends with, "all this will come true unless we choose to reverse it." If you read it backwards, each line has an opposite meaning, and it becomes happy.

Reference: (https://genius.com/Jonathan-reed-the-lost-generation-annotated)

196.

March 6th is the annual sacred High Holy Day of Dudeism, "The Day of The Dude". Dudeism is a religion, philosophy, or lifestyle inspired by "The Dude", the protagonist of 1998 film, The Big Lebowski.

Reference: (https://wikipedia.org/wiki/Dudeism)

197.

Edwarda O'Hara survived in a coma from the age of 16 until her death 42 years later. She was cared for by her family the entire time.

Reference: (https://en.wikipedia.org/wiki/Edwarda_O'Bara)

198.

There is a social Huntsman Spider. Native to Australia, they live in colonies of up to 300, share prey, and aggressively attack and cannibalize outsiders. They were also widely used in the movie "Arachnophobia" and at the start of "Spider-Man."

Reference: (https://en.wikipedia.org/wiki/Delena_cancerides)

199.

Rjukan, a Norwegian town that experiences 7 months of no direct sunlight, built large mirrors on a nearby mountainside to reflect the sun and illuminate the town square.

Reference: (https://en.wikipedia.org/wiki/Rjukan)

200.

Scientists discovered through gene editing how to create a spider with 10 legs.

Reference: (https://en.wikipedia.org/wiki/Antennapedia#Antennapedia_in_arachnids)

201.

There is a bar on a Wisconsin island where people have been doing Angostura shots for nearly a century.

Reference: (https://www.atlasobscura.com/articles/washington-island-wisconsin-bitters-shots)

202.

New York City has liquid nitrogen tanks out in the open on sidewalks.

Reference: (https://www.youtube.com/watch?v=juZqGU9iuq0)

203.

Hundreds of Missouri River steamboats sunk in the early 1800's are buried underground because the river path has shifted. Landowners along the river are unaware of the millions of dollars of treasure buried beneath their land, as many of these boats were loaded with supplies.

Reference: (http://www.moexplorer.com/?p=33)

204.

The largest gold coin minted is the Australian Kangaroo One Tonne Gold Coin, weighing one metric ton, over 31 inches in diameter, 4 inches wide, with a face value of AUD 1,000,000, and gold value of over USD 42,500,000.

Reference: (https://www.perthmint.com/1-tonne-gold-coin.aspx)

205.

Blue LED lights are installed at certain Tokyo train stations to deter suicides. Research found the presence of blue lights resulted in an 84% decrease in suicides. Although the exact reason is unknown, it is theorized blue light has a positive calming effect on mood.

Reference: (https://nextcity.org/daily/entry/how-blue-lights-on-train-platforms-combat-tokyos-suicide-epidemic)

206.

Peanuts grow underground and not on trees.

Reference: (http://www.auntrubyspeanuts.com/howgrow)

207.

In 1969, Neiman Marcus listed a $10,000 kitchen computer in its Christmas Catalog, which came with a cookbook, apron, and a 2 week programming course. None were sold.

Reference: (https://www.wired.com/2012/11/kitchen-computer/)

208.

The actress who played Carol Stills on "The Office" has been married to Steve Carrel since 1995.

Reference: (https://en.wikipedia.org/wiki/Nancy_Carell#Personal_life)

209.

The Subaru logo represents the stars in Pleiades constellation which is known as "Subaru" in Japanese.

Reference: (http://thenewswheel.com/behind-badge-what-do-six-stars-subarus-logo-signify/)

210.

A tiny village inside the Korean DMZ buses in students to its highly in-demand elementary school. It even has a waiting list of over 50 children.

Reference: (https://www.stripes.com/news/pacific/korea/school-in-dmz-s-freedom-village-becomes-coveted-learning-spot-for-s-koreans-1.152120#.VDgCT7nbHws.tumblr)

211.

Andrew Lincoln's name at birth was Andrew James Clutterbuck.

Reference: (https://en.wikipedia.org/wiki/Andrew_Lincoln)

212.

Before the Battle of Midway in World War II, the Allies sent a message to Midway that they were "low on water." Intercepted Japanese messages stated that their next objective was low on water, giving Allies an advantage at the battle.

Reference: (https://en.wikipedia.org/wiki/Battle_of_Midway#Allied_code-breaking)

213.

The city of Lima got its name because the Spanish mispronounced the name of the river in the area when they discovered it.

Reference: (https://www.britannica.com/place/Lima)

214.

The piece of music most associated with the circus is called "Entry of the Gladiators".

Reference: (https://www.youtube.com/watch?v=_B0CyOAO8y0)

215.

Brigham Young's, founder of the Mormon University, son, Brigham Morris Young, was a female impersonator who performed under the stage name of Madam Pattirini and had a falsetto so convincing that many were shocked to find out they weren't a woman.

Reference: (https://www.madampattirini.com/)

216.

North Korea has their own scoring system for basketball games. 3 points for a dunk, 4 points for a typical 3 pointer that is all net, 8 points for a basket in the final 3 seconds, and minus one point for a missed free throw.

Reference: (https://deadspin.com/5988085/north-korea-invented-its-own-totally-different-way-of-scoring-basketball-games)

217.

Some Africans hunt albino people because their bones supposedly bring good luck, happiness and wealth.

Reference: (https://amp.cnn.com/cnn/2016/06/07/africa/africa-albino-hunted-bones-malawi/index.html)

218.

Corn is part of the grass family.

Reference: (http://www.naturemuseum.org/the-museum/blog/is-corn-a-grass)

219.

The writers of "It's Always Sunny In Philadelphia" had never written a script before the show. They picked up writing just to create the show.

Reference: (https://www.youtube.com/watch?v=J328SSYQOJs)

220.

Coco Chanel was a Nazi secret agent and used it, first, to free her nephew from a German prisoner-of-war camp and later to take control of her perfume empire away from the Jewish Wertheimer brothers.

Reference: (http://www.nytimes.com/2011/09/04/books/review/sleeping-with-the-enemy-coco-chanels-secret-war-by-hal-vaughan-book-review.htmlhttps://www.nytimes.com/2011/09/04/books/review/sleeping-with-the-enemy-coco-chanels-secret-war-by-hal-vaughan-book-review.html)

221.

Bucks, male deer, shed their horns every year.

Reference: (https://www.grandviewoutdoors.com/big-game-hunting/why-do-deer-shed-their-antlers/)

222.

Practicing a professional discipline without a license may be legal in some jurisdictions. For example, nine U.S. states have passed health freedom laws that protect alternative practitioners such as herbalists from prosecution for "practicing medicine without a license."

Reference: (https://en.wikipedia.org/wiki/Practicing_without_a_license)

223.

Four of the elements in the Periodic Table are named after Ytterby, a village in Sweden. They are Yttrium, Terbium, Erbium, and Ytterbium.

Reference: (https://en.wikipedia.org/wiki/List_of_chemical_element_name_etymologies)

224.

The so-called "Whiskey fungus" is a fungus that is found in and around warehouses where whiskey is aged. It feeds on the ethanol vapors released as the liquor ages.

Reference: (https://munchies.vice.com/en_us/article/78dyqb/kentuckys-whiskey-fungus-problem-is-out-of-control)

225.

Diane Warren is the Roger Deakins of songwriting. She has been nominated nine times for Best Original Song at the Oscars but has never won.

Reference: (https://en.wikipedia.org/wiki/Diane_Warren#Academy_Awards)

226.

18th century stereotype of the "lazy southerner" was caused by widespread hookworm infections, which caused poor southerners to be lethargic, malnourished, stunted, and mentally retarded.

Reference: (http://www.pbs.org/wgbh/nova/next/nature/how-a-worm-gave-the-south-a-bad-name/)

227.

Poundbury is a town in England build based upon the design ideas of Prince Charles. He notoriously hated post-war town planning, as a result, Poundbury is more "traditional" in style.

Reference: (https://en.wikipedia.org/wiki/Poundbury)

228.

A traditional council chooses the King of Swaziland's first 2 wives, then he picks a woman from every clan in the country and marries them once they become pregnant. When the king dies, the council declares one of his wives who displayed good character as the "Great Wife"; her son becomes king.

Reference: (https://en.wikipedia.org/wiki/Succession_to_the_Swazi_throne)

229.

America's own supervolcano, at Yellowstone National Park, is rocking in one of the largest earthquake swarms ever recorded there. Its super-eruptions tend to occur every 600,000 to 800,000 years; last one was 600,000 years ago.

Reference: (http://www.newsweek.com/yellowstone-supervolcano-earthquake-swarm-longest-ever-recorded-677387)

230.

There was a unit of mass known as a Pood in Russia and it is equal to 36.11 pounds.

Reference: (https://en.wikipedia.org/wiki/Pood)

231.

In the Philippines, there is a game played by the youth called "Spider Fighting" where you find a spider, and have it fight against other spiders on a stick.

Reference: (https://www.youtube.com/watch?v=pKOhYljSWJo&t=523s)

232.

Johann Elser was a German carpenter who almost killed Adolf Hitler and most of the top Nazi leaders shortly before the outbreak of World War II. He worked alone to construct and plant a bomb that went off just 13 minutes too late. He was a Christian motivated by a sense that millions would soon die.

Reference: (https://en.wikipedia.org/wiki/Johann_Georg_Elser)

233.

The ancient Roman Colosseum had a retractable roof.

Reference: (http://www.the-colosseum.net/architecture/novavelarium.htm)

234.

James Madison wrote letters to himself, both as George Washington and as Congress.

Reference: (https://newrepublic.com/article/131552/spirit-89)

235.

Aleksandar Shalamanov represented Bulgaria as an alpine skier in the 1960 Winter Olympics and as a footballer in the 1966 and 1970 FIFA World Cups.

Reference: (https://en.wikipedia.org/wiki/Aleksandar_Shalamanov)

236.

NASA had detailed plans to get humans to Mars by as early as 1981, but the mission didn't get enough support from the Nixon administration and was shelved.

Reference: (https://www.wired.com/2012/06/the-last-manned-mars-plan-1971/)

237.

Since 1932, Thailand has had 19 coups attempts, 12 of them successful.

Reference: (http://www.cbc.ca/news/world/thailand-s-19th-coup-underscores-country-s-fatal-flaw-1.2658846)

238.

The crab meat commonly found in California Rolls is actually made out of fish paste and flavored like crab.

Reference: (https://www.businessinsider.com.au/imitation-crab-meat-ingredients-explained-2017-5?r=US&IR=T)

239.

"Tunnel Rats" were allied soldiers in Vietnam that performed underground search and destroy missions, often times with just a pistol.

Reference: (https://en.wikipedia.org/wiki/Tunnel_rat)

240.

In 2015, a Japanese tourist died from falling down a staircase while trying to take a selfie at the Taj Mahal.

Reference: (https://nypost.com/2015/09/23/more-people-die-from-selfies-than-shark-attacks/)

241.

Joseph Stalin's real name was Iosif Vissarionovich Dzhugashvili. He decided to change his name to Stalin in 1902, meaning "steel" in Russian, which he believed would make him appear tough.

Reference: (https://www.biography.com/people/joseph-stalin-9491723)

242.

Between 1909 and 1911, what would eventually become the U.S. Air Force consisted of one guy at Fort Sam with the crashed plane that killed his comrade, that he repaired himself and taught himself to fly. He then crashed it again.

Reference: (https://en.wikipedia.org/wiki/Aeronautical_Division,_U.S._Signal_Corps)

243.

Bacteria in your gut make you calm.

Reference: (https://www.popularmechanics.com/science/health/a7235/how-probiotic-microbes-control-your-mind/)

244.

After the French Revolution, the newly formed government established a calendar with 1792 as the Year 1; months, days and hours on a 10 based system, and new names for the months, such as Floreal and Vendémiaire.

Reference: (http://www.prisonersofeternity.co.uk/french-revolutionary-calendar/)

245.

In the early 20th century, Kansas sent women to prisons for having STDs or even seeming like the "type of woman" who might have them.

Reference: (https://timeline.com/amp/p/a0a9c853e6e4)

246.

In 1988, sideshow performer Grady Stiles, also known as "Lobster Boy", killed his daughter's fiancé. Never jailed, he remained abusive. In 1992, his first wife, Mary Teresa hired a 17 year old sideshow performer, Chris Wyant, to kill Stiles, though Stiles was ultimately killed by a neighbor in 1996.

Reference: (https://en.wikipedia.org/wiki/Grady_Stiles)

247.

Hákarl are buried, fermented and dried Greenland shark; it's a traditional dish of Iceland. It is heavy in ammonia, giving it a putrid smell, and people who try it the first time often involuntarily trigger the gag reflex.

Reference: (https://www.worldatlas.com/articles/icelandic-cuisine-hakarl-iceland-fermented-shark.html)

248.

The U.K. was the only European country besides Spain with an organized fascist movement that survived World War II. After the war, the British Union of Fascists continued operating as it had prior to the war.

Reference: (https://www.thehistorypress.co.uk/articles/fighting-fascists-battling-oswald-mosley-s-blackshirts/)

249.

The first KFC was not in Kentucky, but in Salt Lake City.

Reference: (https://www.deseretnews.com/article/700217162/Story-of-first-KFC-shows-anything-can-happen.html?pg=all)

250.

The Book of the Wars of the Lord is a non-canonical book referenced in the Bible which has been completely lost.

Reference: (https://en.wikipedia.org/wiki/Book_of_the_Wars_of_the_Lord)

251.

There are more people who have learned English as a second language than there are native speakers.

Reference: (https://en.wikipedia.org/wiki/English_language)

252.

"Cloaca" is an art installation by Wim Delvoye which literally digests food into feces.

Reference: (https://wimdelvoye.be/work/cloaca/cloaca-original-1/)

253.

Lee Harvey Oswald was not arrested for killing John F. Kennedy, he was arrested for murdering J. D. Tippit.

Reference: (https://www.cbsnews.com/news/jfk-assassination-suspect-lee-harvey-oswald-is-arrested-then-gunned-down/)

254.

An Israeli pilot landed an F15 fighter after a midair collision tore off his wing.

Reference: (https://www.youtube.com/watch?v=MzvVd-f71dM&feature=youtu.be&t=16m33s)

255.

Morality changes in a foreign language. Foreign language learners give more utilitarian judgments in moral predicaments than native speakers. A weaker emotional connection to your second language could mean a loosening of your morals.

Reference: (https://www.scientificamerican.com/article/how-morality-changes-in-a-foreign-language/)

256.

Pauley Pavilion opened in 1965. The opening game featured its 2-time defending champion, top-ranked men's varsity basketball team. It was annihilated by the UCLA Freshmen team.

Reference: (http://articles.latimes.com/1990-11-27/sports/sp-5543_1_freshman-team)

257.

The Sun perfectly aligns with 5 ellipses in 5 pillars, representing each branch of the military, illuminating the United States Seal, every year on Veterans Day at exactly 11:11am.

Reference: (https://nerdist.com/the-sun-perfectly-illuminates-a-veterans-day-memorial-each-year/)

258.

Soviet leader Joseph Stalin had a secret laboratory in which he and other scientists analyzed the stool samples of Mao Zedong and other perceived "enemies" to understand the inner-workings of their brains.

Reference: (https://didyouknowfacts.com/joseph-stalin-secret-sht-laboratory-used-creep-mao/)

259.

There was such a thing as a Groom of the Stool, a servant that would assist a king during his visit to the toilet. The servants would often be involved in important decisions due to the intimate relationship they had with their employer.

Reference: (https://en.wikipedia.org/wiki/Groom_of_the_Stool)

260.

John Wojtowicz used scenes from "The Godfather" as inspiration of how to pull off his infamous 1972 bank robbery. A movie was made based on the robbery called "Dog Day Afternoon", it starred Al Pacino and John Cazale, both famous for starring in "The Godfather".

Reference: (https://en.wikipedia.org/wiki/Salvatore_Naturale#The_robbery)

261.

The unique snare drum sound in Fine Young Cannibals' "She Drives Me Crazy" was created by recording a snare drum normally. A speaker was then placed on top of the drum, and a microphone below. The original recording of the snare drum part was played back through the speaker and re-recorded.

Reference: (https://en.wikipedia.org/wiki/She_Drives_Me_Crazy#Background_and_recording)

262.

Naturally aspirated engines are usually derated 2.5 percent in horsepower per 1,000 feet above mean sea level, a tremendous penalty at the 10,000 feet which several U.S. and Canada railroads operate, and this can amount to a 25 percent power loss. Turbocharging effectively eliminates this derating.

Reference: (https://en.wikipedia.org/wiki/EMD_645)

263.

There are actually eight continents, with the eighth, being nearly 95% submerged, called Zealandia.

Reference: (http://www.geosociety.org/gsatoday/archive/27/3/article/GSATG321A.1.htm)

264.

Green bell peppers are just unripe versions of red peppers.

Reference: (http://www.huffingtonpost.ca/entry/difference-between-peppers_us_56def9efe4b03a405679fe7c)

265.

Forest bathing, an ancient Japanese tradition, has several scientifically proven anti-anxiety and heart-related benefits.

Reference: (http://ponderwall.com/index.php/2016/02/11/forests-air-has-an-excellent-therapeutic-effect/)

266.

The smallest fruit in the world is the size of a grain of salt.

Reference: (https://www2.palomar.edu/users/warmstrong/plfeb96.htm)

267.

There is a high school in Australia which offered every freshmen to study aboard in China for 5 weeks. They even have a dedicated campus in Nanjing, China.

Reference: (https://www.caulfieldgs.vic.edu.au/quality-learning/internationalism/)

268.

Sperm counts among western men have halved in the last 40 years.

Reference: (https://www.theguardian.com/lifeandstyle/2017/jul/25/sperm-counts-among-western-men-have-halved-in-last-40-years-study)

269.

If you own a Rolls Royce, you can send your chauffeur to the Rolls Royce headquarters in Goodwood, England to be trained to drive a Rolls Royce under the "White Glove" driver training program.

Reference: (http://blog.rolls-roycemotorcarsraleigh.com/rolls-royce-launches-new-white-glove-driver-training-program/)

270.

There's a three-player chess game using an hexagonal board.

Reference: (https://interestingengineering.com/three-player-chess-just-crazy-sounds)

271.

Between 1809 and 1981, the municipality of Huéscar in Granada, Spain, was at war with Denmark as a result of the Napoleonic wars over Spain. However, not a single shot was fired during the 172 years of war, and nobody was killed or injured.

Reference: (https://en.wikipedia.org/wiki/Province_of_Granada)

272.

Worcestershire Sauce is made, in part, from 18-month-old fermented anchovies.

Reference: (http://www.huffingtonpost.ca/entry/what-is-worcestershire-sauce_us_57ac8af8e4b0db3be07d5b45)

273.

Treasury Street, one of the narrowest streets in the United States, was allegedly created to protect against pirates.

Reference: (https://www.atlasobscura.com/places/treasury-street)

274.

"Boneless Pork Rectums" are a real product, and inverting them is a time-consuming process.

Reference: (http://wmbriggs.com/post/2926/)

275.

The man that created Wonder Woman was a psychologist that helped invent the polygraph machine, which is why Wonder Woman has the Lasso of Truth. He also believed women were emotionally superior to men and that the U.S. would one day be a matriarchy.

Reference: (https://wikipedia.org/wiki/William_Moulton_Marston)

276.

Upon the death of Intharacha, King of Ayutthaya, his two sons fought to the death aboard elephants. The throne then went to the younger brother.

Reference: (https://en.wikipedia.org/wiki/Intharacha_(king_of_Ayutthaya))

277.

In winter, dogs with white or light-colored fur will often lose pigment in their noses, leaving a pink or light brown streak in the middle. This is called "Snow Nose" or "Winter Nose."

Reference: (https://naturaldogcompany.com/articles/pink-dog-nose-snow-nose-is-not-just-a-winter-condition/)

278.

Researchers have experimented with using Wasabi vapor to create silent fire alarms for the deaf.

Reference: (http://inventorspot.com/articles/wasabi_silent_fire_alarm_alerts__11514)

279.

Lightbulbs were originally made with cardboard paper or bamboo as filament.

Reference: (https://en.wikipedia.org/wiki/Incandescent_light_bulb#Filament)

280.

Attacking your avocado tree can shock it into bearing fruit.

Reference: (http://www.fruitexpert.co.uk/growingavocados.html)

281.

Giant "zipper" trucks move the lanes of certain highways every day.

Reference: (https://en.wikipedia.org/wiki/Barrier_transfer_machine)

282.

Japanese role playing games like Final Fantasy came from the Western role playing games Wizardy and Ultima.

Reference: (https://kotaku.com/the-dungeons-and-dragons-session-that-became-a-real-lif-1691643499)

283.

It took a dozen people at a time to operate Johnny 5, the robot in the Short Circuit movie.

Reference: (https://io9.gizmodo.com/16-things-you-probably-never-knew-about-the-short-circu-1727251497)

284.

Prince Harry of Wales served in Afghanistan for ten weeks in 2007 and 2008. Subsequently, he was pulled out of the country after an Australian newspaper reported on his presence in the Helmand Province of Afghanistan.

Reference: (https://en.wikipedia.org/wiki/Prince_Harry#Military_career)

285.

The aging paradox states that people get happier as they get older. People in their 60s and higher generally report higher levels of happiness and life satisfaction than those who are younger.

Reference: (http://www.latimes.com/science/sciencenow/la-sci-sn-older-people-happier-20160824-snap-story.html)

286.

Fried beer won the most creative Big Tex Prize at the 2010 Texas State Fair.

Reference: (http://www.dallasobserver.com/restaurants/fried-beer-takes-the-prize-at-state-fair-7029621)

287.

Oscar Hammerstein II is the only person named Oscar to win an Oscar.

Reference: (http://awardsdatabase.oscars.org/)

288.

A survey by SunTrust Mortgage found that a third of millennial home owners said they were influenced by the need to have space for a dog. Their dog was the third most commonly cited reason, coming above children and marriage.

Reference: (http://time.com/money/4876151/millenials-homes-dogs-children-marriages/)

289.

Lt. Col. Percy Fawcett, with his eldest son, disappeared into the jungle of Brazil looking for the lost city of “Z”.

Reference: (https://en.wikipedia.org/wiki/Percy_Fawcett)

290.

The TV theme song for “Beakman’s World" was composed by Mark Mothersbaugh from Devo.

Reference: (https://en.wikipedia.org/wiki/Beakman%27s_World)

291.

A snowflake is a mineral.

Reference: (https://www.e-education.psu.edu/earth520/node/1688)

292.

Boxing star Vasyl Lomachenko took traditional Ukrainian ballet classes for 4 years.

Reference: (http://www.espn.co.uk/boxing/story/_/id/21681715/training-just-piece-puzzle-vasiliy-lomachenko-lomachenko-vs-rigondeaux-espn)

293.

San Diego Zoo maintains a so-called "frozen zoo", a facility in which they preserve DNA from rare and near-extinct species.

Reference: (https://en.wikipedia.org/wiki/San_Diego_Zoo#Conservation)

294.

Eight per cent of Britons have never been to London.

Reference: (https://www.telegraph.co.uk/travel/news/Average-Briton-has-visited-seven-countries/)

295.

"Thou" used to be informal while "you" was formal.

Reference: (http://www.shakespeareswords.com/thou-and-you)

296.

A Blue Moon isn't the only named Moon; for example, the Full Moon of January is a "Wolf Moon".

Reference: (https://www.nationalgeographic.com/science/space/solar-system/full-moon/)

297.

In 2017, officers from Devon and Cornwall, United Kingdom commandeered a double-decker bus, using the top deck to monitor motorists illegally using their mobile phones while driving. In two days, they caught 39 drivers using their phones and 36 not wearing a seatbelt.

Reference: (https://www.telegraph.co.uk/news/2017/03/27/police-stake-motorists-top-deck-bus-catch-mobile-phone-offenders/)

298.

Fox initially did not want Gillian Anderson in the role of Dana Scully on "The X-Files" because they thought she wasn't hot enough.

Reference: (https://en.wikipedia.org/wiki/Gillian_Anderson)

299.

Before he was a famous musician, Johnny Cash was a military code breaker for the U.S. Air Force. He worked as a as a Morse Intercept Operator in Germany, handling the hardest jobs, intercepting Russian intelligence and deciphering code transmissions. He copied the 1st news of Stalin's death.

Reference: (http://themalestrom.com/before-they-were-famous/)

300.

An 8th grader tried to pay for her lunch with a 2 Dollar Bill that had been given to her by her grandmother. The police were called because the school thought it was fake, and investigated where the bill had been obtained. In the end, the bill was real.

Reference: (http://abc13.com/news/lunchroom-lunacy-isd-cops-investigate-fake-money/1314203/)

301.

Taco Bell was founded by Glen Bell who watched long lines of customers at a Mexican restaurant. He ate there regularly, attempting to reverse-engineer the taco recipe, and eventually persuaded the owners to show him how they were prepared. With this knowledge, he opened a stand selling tacos.

Reference: (https://en.wikipedia.org/wiki/Taco_Bell#History)

302.

General Douglas MacArthur wanted to use atomic bombs in the Korean War.

Reference: (https://www.airspacemag.com/military-aviation/how-korean-war-almost-went-nuclear-180955324/)

303.

The WASP is a 60 mile per hour flying platform developed by the U.S. Army.

Reference: (https://en.wikipedia.org/wiki/Williams_X-Jet)

304.

Erasmus was a theologian who compiled the first Greek translation of the Christian Bible. He caused an outcry when his version didn't include the trinity. It turns out that the trinity isn't found in the earliest Greek manuscripts and he claimed he could find no source to support it.

Reference: (https://bible.org/article/textual-problem-1-john-57-8)

305.

Giraffes are technically kosher by definition but still would not be eaten because they are not traditional and prohibitive on slaughtering.

Reference: (https://ohr.edu/3184)

306.

Ketchup was once sold as medicine.

Reference: (https://www.ripleys.com/weird-news/ketchup-was-once-used-as-medicine/)

307.

A well-mated and well-fed queen bee can lay about 1,500 to 2,000 eggs per day during the spring build-up, which is about one egg every 20 to 30 seconds. This is more than her own body weight in eggs every day.

Reference: (https://www.beeplusmanukahoney.com/the-queen-bee)

308.

Pierre Sprey helped design the F-16 and A-10 fighter planes. He also helped record "Jesus Walks" for Kanye West.

Reference: (https://en.wikipedia.org/wiki/Pierre_Sprey)

309.

There are two Antioch's in the New Testament, though the Syrian Antioch was by far more important.

Reference: (https://www.simplybible.com/f99e.htm)

310.

Snoop Dogg tried to rent the entire country of Liechtenstein for a music video shoot.

Reference: (https://nypost.com/2010/07/01/snoop-dogg-wants-to-rent-entire-country/)

311.

Researchers found that beards were only more attractive if they were uncommon. In a study, if researchers showed a single bearded man amongst many shaved men, the bearded person was ranked as more attractive. If shown amongst other bearded men, it lost its benefit.

Reference: (http://www.cbc.ca/news/technology/beards-are-sexier-when-they-re-uncommon-study-shows-1.2612259)

312.

The hyena is not a canine species. Instead, it's part of the filiform suborder and thus closer to a cat-like species.

Reference: (https://en.wikipedia.org/wiki/Hyena)

313.

The continuously ringing bells at Oxford University have been going since 1840 with batteries no one wants to open to see the contents of until the bell finally ceases to ring.

Reference: (https://www.smithsonianmag.com/smart-news/mystery-continuously-functioning-battery-1840-180954028/)

314.

Ancient Babylonian men were the first to manicure their nails. The coloring of their nails was used to signify their social class within society. Black signified you were of the upper classes while green signified you were a commoner. They even created manicure kits to aid the practice.

Reference: (https://www.marieclaire.com/beauty/makeup/a9570/history-of-manicures/)

315.

Plumpy'Nut is a peanut based paste, made for treatment of severe acute malnutrition. It can alleviate a starving child from impending illness or death.

Reference: (https://en.wikipedia.org/wiki/Plumpy%27nut)

316.

Ust-Nera is one of the coldest permanently inhabited regions on Earth, where temperatures can go as low as -50ºC, or -58ºF, in winter.

Reference: (https://en.wikipedia.org/wiki/Ust-Nera)

317.

In 2016, a group of hackers almost stole $1 billion from the New York Federal Reserve, but were discovered when they spelled "foundation" as "fandation" in money request transcripts. They still managed to get away with $81 million.

Reference: (https://www.reuters.com/article/us-usa-fed-bangladesh-typo-insight/how-a-hackers-typo-helped-stop-a-billion-dollar-bank-heist-idUSKCN0WC0TC)

318.

Jim Becker, a Packers fan Hall-of-Famer, routinely sold his blood to buy season tickets, which inadvertently saved his life when he was found to have Hemochromatosis, a genetic disorder that leads to toxic iron deposition in the body, and an early death. The only treatment is bloodletting.

Reference: (http://abcnews.go.com/Health/MensHealth/football-fan-paying-tickets-saved-fatal-disease/story?id=10109129)

319.

Paul Alexander is one of the last few Polio survivors. He's confined to an Iron Lung and paralyzed from the neck down, yet managed to graduate from law school and wrote his memoir using only his mouth.

Reference: (https://www.youtube.com/watch?v=gplA6pq9cOs)

320.

Between 108 BC and 1911 AD, there were no fewer than 1,828 major famines in China, or one nearly every year in one or another province with the severity of each famine varying greatly.

Reference: (https://en.wikipedia.org/wiki/List_of_famines)

321.

102-year-old cyclist Robert Marchand held the 100-plus category one-hour record of 24 kilometers and 251 meters until he broke his own record at the age of 102, riding 26 kilometers and 927 meters in one hour.

Reference: (http://www.cyclingnews.com/news/102-year-old-robert-marchand-beats-own-hour-record/)

322.

Tutankhamun was buried with an erect penis.

Reference: (http://www.discovery-zone.com/ancient-mystery-solved-tutankhamun-buried-erect-penis/)

323.

During the Crosby by-election in the United Kingdom in 1981, a 22-year old candidate legally changed his name from John Desmond Lewis to Tarquin Fin-tim-lin-bin-whin-bim-lim-bus-stop-

F'tang-F'tang-Olé-Biscuitbarrel, in homage to a character from a Monty Python's Flying Circus sketch.

Reference: (https://en.wikipedia.org/wiki/Crosby_by-election,_1981)

324.

There is a species of lemur that is named after British comedian John Cleese. The scientist who discovered it named it after Cleese because of his fondness for lemurs, and his efforts at protecting and preserving them.

Reference: (http://www.foxnews.com/story/2005/11/11/lemur-species-named-after-john-cleese.html)

325.

A lottery scratcher in England was cancelled because too many customers could not figure out which is the higher of two negative numbers.

Reference: (https://www.manchestereveningnews.co.uk/news/greater-manchester-news/cool-cash-card-confusion-1009701)

326.

Easter, and therefore also Whitsun, Ascension and the Dutch Carnaval, depends on the first full moon after the spring equinox, so after March 21st. Easter can be as early as March 22nd and April 25th at its latest.

Reference: (https://www.christianitytoday.com/history/2008/august/why-does-easters-date-wander.html)

327.

American Airlines once flew the wrong plane from Los Angeles to Honolulu. The plane lacked certification to fly for long periods where there are no emergency landing alternatives nearby.

Reference: (https://www.theverge.com/2015/9/13/9320061/american-airlines-accidentally-used-the-wrong-plane-to-fly-to-hawaii)

328.

Silly String has military usage in the detection of tripwires. The string would settle onto the ground in areas without tripwires, but catch on to any that is present. The silly string reveals the wire, but it will not set it off due to its light weight.

Reference: (https://en.wikipedia.org/wiki/Silly_String#Military_use)

329.

Earwax, also known as cerumen, is actually good for you. It protects you from not only dust, but also micro-organisms.

Reference: (https://www.healthline.com/health/earwax-buildup)

330.

We have more microbes in our body, mostly in our gut, than all of our body cells combined.

Reference: (http://www.microbiomeinstitute.org/blog/2016/1/20/how-many-bacterial-vs-human-cells-are-in-the-body)

331.

Quantum tunneling is responsible for many of the factors necessary for life, including the formation of water in space, nuclear fusion in the Sun, photosynthesis, and DNA mutation and repair.

Reference: (https://www.ncbi.nlm.nih.gov/pmc/articles/PMC3768233/)

332.

Project X-Ray was a plan to drop bombs full of small bats, each attached with timed incendiary bombs, on Japan. The nocturnal bats would seek shelter from the Sun into Japanese wooden houses and spread fire throughout the city.

Reference: (https://en.wikipedia.org/wiki/Bat_bomb)

333.

Hojunmaru was a Japanese fishing ship with three survivors who ran aground in what is now Washington State in 1834, making the first recorded contact between Native Americans and Asians.

Reference: (http://www.historylink.org/File/9065)

334.

Charles Darwin tested a dog who recognized him after an absence of five years and two days.

Reference: (http://charles-darwin.classic-literature.co.uk/the-descent-of-man/ebook-page-51.asp)

335.

Alysia Rissling, born November 16, 1988, is a Canadian bobsledder. In 2015, she was the pilot for the first ever all-woman team in an official four-man bobsleigh race after the event became gender neutral.

Reference: (https://en.wikipedia.org/wiki/Alysia_Rissling)

336.

New Mexico's disorderly conduct law includes rules that prohibit dueling.

Reference: (http://statelaws.findlaw.com/new-mexico-law/new-mexico-disorderly-conduct-laws.html)

337.

The Sphinx of Giza has a KFC around 200 meters away from it.

Reference: (http://twistedsifter.com/2014/03/the-pyramids-of-giza-from-kfc-egypt/)

338.

Max Kellerman's brother, Sam Kellerman, was killed by a boxer named the Harlem Hammer with a hammer. The boxer is also infamous for the dirtiest cheap shot in boxing history.

Reference:(https://wikipedia.org/wiki/James_Butler_(boxer)#Murder_of_Sam_Kellerman_and_conviction)

339.

The creator of Anti-Monopoly, basically the opposite of Monopoly, was sued by Parker Brothers in 1974.

Reference: (https://en.wikipedia.org/wiki/Anti-Monopoly)

340.

Fiestaware kitchenware made up until the 1970's and Coleman Lanterns made into the mid-1990's emit significant amounts of radiation above background. A red Fiestaware plate from the period is about 20% uranium and Coleman used thorium in their lantern mantels.

Reference: (https://www.vaughns-1-pagers.com/science/geiger-counters-compare.htm)

341.

Belly buttons can get itchy, crusty, and even catch an infection.

Reference: (https://share.upmc.com/2015/07/how-to-keep-your-bellybutton-navel-clean-the-right-way/)

342.

The Ford Ranger mid-size truck will once again be sold in the U.S., starting with the 2019 model.

Reference: (https://www.caranddriver.com/features/2019-ford-ranger-25-cars-worth-waiting-for-feature)

343.

Henry Worsley attempted to cross Antarctica solo and on foot in 2015 and came within 30 miles of his goal before he had to call for help. He died soon after being rescued.

Reference: (https://www.npr.org/sections/thetwo-way/2016/01/25/464274120/explorer-dies-just-short-of-goal-crossing-the-antarctic-unaided)

344.

In 1997, at the age of 33, Guillermo Del Toro was given a $30 million budget from Miramax Films to shoot another film, Mimic. During this time, his father was kidnapped in Guadalajara. Del Toro's family had to pay twice the amount originally asked for as a ransom.

Reference: (https://en.wikipedia.org/wiki/Guillermo_del_Toro)

345.

The Unknown Soldier Memorial in Egypt is, perhaps unsurprisingly, pyramid-shaped.

Reference: (https://en.wikipedia.org/wiki/Unknown_Soldier_Memorial_(Egypt))

346.

The characterization of Jesus as a warrior is derived from the syncretization of Christianity and Germanic Paganism to encourage conversion.

Reference: (https://en.wikipedia.org/wiki/Germanic_Christianity#Characteristics)

347.

Those who empathize with the suffering of others predominantly by emotion-sharing rather than solution seeking have been shown to be less likely to alleviate that suffering by exchanging places with the sufferer.

Reference: (http://nautil.us/issue/35/Boundaries/how-to-avoid-empathy-burnout)

348.

Conway Twitty recorded a Russian version of "Hello Darlin'," a number one country hit in 1970, for the Apollo-Soyuz Test Project, the first joint space mission between the Soviet Union and the U.S. It was broadcast to the world from space as a gift to the Soviets from the Americans.

Reference: (https://history.nasa.gov/astp/music.htm)

349.

In 1937, in order to increase union recognition, women on strike would pull workers out of their cabs on the way to work, strip them, and spank them in the streets.

Reference: (https://cdnc.ucr.edu/cgi-bin/cdnc?a=d&d=MT19370119.2.17)

350.

Gerry and the Pacemakers, a band from Liverpool, scored three consecutive number 1 hits in the U.K. They were also managed by Brian Epstein and produced by George Martin, just like that other famous band from Liverpool.

Reference: (https://en.wikipedia.org/wiki/Gerry_and_the_Pacemakers)

351.

During World War II, Eddie Chapman, or as people during World War II called him, "Agent Zigzag", leaked falsified information to Germany by reporting that their bombs were hitting the intended target, Central London, but in reality they were undershooting at several kilometers and missed every time.

Reference: (https://www.sunderlandecho.com/lifestyle/retro/sunderland-spy-won-the-praise-of-hitler-1-7452336)

352.

An NGO called APOPO trains rats to sniff out landmines in Africa.

Reference: (https://en.wikipedia.org/wiki/Giant_pouched_rat)

353.

In 2005, the USA was the top horse meat producing country and China was the top horse meat consuming country.

Reference: (https://en.wikipedia.org/wiki/Horse_meat)

354.

In 1993, comic "For Better or For Worse" ran a story about a gay character coming out to his parents. It was criticized by hundreds of fans, over 100 newspapers cancelled the strip over it, and even parts of the gay community were against it.

Reference: (https://en.wikipedia.org/wiki/For_Better_or_For_Worse#Lawrence_comes_out)

355.

The movie "The Iron Giant," produced by Pete Townsend, was originally planned as a rock opera.

Reference: (http://ultimateclassicrock.com/iron-giant)

356.

Penn Jillette could have played Rolo Haynes in the Black Museum episode of "Black Mirror."

Reference: (https://en.wikipedia.org/wiki/Black_Museum_(Black_Mirror)#Production)

357.

Julie Andrews, of "Song of Music" fame, lost her singing voice after a botched surgery in 1997.

Reference: (https://en.wikipedia.org/wiki/Julie_Andrews#Loss_of_singing_voice)

358.

The Japanese soft drink Ramune was invented before Coke.

Reference: (https://taiken.co/single/ramune-the-japanese-summer-soda/)

359.

Staten Island's deer population increased 9,000% in 9 years.

Reference: (http://www.silive.com/news/2017/04/staten_island_deer_herd_size.html)

360.

Scots, one of Scotland's three national languages, is mostly readable to English speakers.

Reference:(http://www.slate.com/blogs/lexicon_valley/2014/08/05/despite_disputes_over_whether_scots_is_separate_language_or_dialect_of_english.html)

361.

From 1997 to 2002, Ford made an electric version of the Ford Ranger, which competed with Chevrolet's S-10 electric truck.

Reference: (https://en.wikipedia.org/wiki/Ford_Ranger_EV)

362.

Nintendo will not allow the creator of Super Mario to bike to work because they consider his safety to be too important.

Reference: (http://www.thisisinsider.com/nintendo-wont-let-super-mario-creator-bike-to-work-2016-7)

363.

The University of South Africa found 18% of laborers believe in the virgin cleansing myth for HIV infections.

Reference: (https://en.wikipedia.org/wiki/Virgin_cleansing_myth#Prevalence)

364.

A Benedictine nun, Dolores Hart, is a voting member for the Oscars and still receives screeners to this day.

Reference: (http://globalsistersreport.org/news/trends/mother-dolores-hart-shares-new-hollywood-memoir-fans-39496)

365.

During the 2005 Jilin chemical plant explosions in China, over 100 tons of pollutants containing benzene and nitrobenzene entered the Songhua River, and the government responded by shutting off the water for the city of Harbin, which has a population of 3.8 million, for five days.

Reference: (https://en.wikipedia.org/wiki/2005_Jilin_chemical_plant_explosions)

366.

In 1950, a cruise ship found a proboscis monkey far out in the South China Sea. Mistaken for a human and brought aboard, it later chose to return to the water.

Reference: (https://blogs.scientificamerican.com/tetrapod-zoology/amazing-swimming-proboscis-monkey-part-i/)

367.

Trees in forests have an underground communication and interaction system driven by fungal networks. "Mother trees" pass on information for best growth patterns and can divert nutrients to trees in need, and they are more likely to pass them on to trees of their own species.

Reference: (https://www.ted.com/speakers/suzanne_simard)

368.

John Tavares, uncle of New York Islanders Captain John Tavares, was also a franchise caliber player, but in lacrosse.

Reference: (https://en.wikipedia.org/wiki/John_Tavares_(lacrosse))

369.

Walt Disney won an honorary Oscar with 7 little Oscars on it, for "Snow White and the 7 Dwarfs."

Reference: (https://www.popsugar.com/smart-living/photo-gallery/38432895/image/38445766/Walt-received-very-unique-honorary-Oscar-Snow-White-Seven-Dwarfs)

370.

Anime character Captain Harlock is a far-right icon among Italian neo-fascists.

Reference: (https://en.wikipedia.org/wiki/Captain_Harlock#Reception_and_cultural_impact)

371.

Legendary jazz musician Charles Mingus developed and promoted a method of training cats to use toilet bowls.

Reference: (http://mingusmingusmingus.com/mingus/cat-traning-program)

372.

In a 2015 poll, 1 in 10 Americans thought it was a mistake for the U.S. to fight in World War II, and another 1 in 10 “didn't know”.

Reference:(https://d25d2506sfb94s.cloudfront.net/cumulus_uploads/document/nm33fk7pqr/econTabReport.pdf#table.74)

373.

Hoary marmots are the largest member of the squirrel family. They can weigh up to 30 pounds.

Reference: (https://en.wikipedia.org/wiki/Hoary_marmot)

374.

37% of Brits think they have a job that is "utterly useless" and the rate is similar in other countries.

Reference: (https://www.weforum.org/agenda/2017/04/why-its-time-to-rethink-the-meaning-of-work/)

375.

Until 2001, almost all American stock exchanges did not use the penny, preferring instead to use fractions such as 1/64 of a dollar in their valuations.

Reference: (https://www.gao.gov/products/GAO-05-535)

376.

Alejandro G. Inarritu has won his fifth Oscar this year, a Special Achievement Academy Award for his virtual reality film project “Flesh and Sand”.

Reference: (https://www.theverge.com/2017/10/27/16562434/alejandro-gonzalez-inarritu-carne-y-arena-oscar-special-award-vr)

377.

Whoopi Goldberg's stage name comes from her incessant farting during rehearsals early in her stage career. Her cast would say that she, "was like a whoopee cushion."

Reference: (https://us.hellomagazine.com/celebrities/2017021036551/whoopi-goldberg-reveals-hilarious-reason-she-got-her-name/)

378.

The "Strange Situation" is a lab procedure used to assess infants' pattern of attachment to their caregiver by introducing an unexpected threat.

Reference: (https://www.tandfonline.com/doi/full/10.1080/14616734.2017.1354040)

379.

Every year, large parts of the North American western coastline turn milky white as millions of herring collectively spray thousands of gallons of semen over their spawning grounds to take part in one of the largest mass-fertilizations of the animal kingdom.

Reference: (https://www.azula.com/herrings-semen-can-be-seen-from-a-helicopter-2476365533.html)

380.

Waffle House uses a special arrangement of condiments on a plate to mark your order for the cook.

Reference: (https://www.youtube.com/watch?v=yhhlCz9AJC4&feature=youtu.be)

381.

In order to prepare for landing the Space Shuttle, affectionately referred to as a "flying brick", astronauts trained in a modified Gulfstream II with the main landing gear down and the engine thrust in reverse.

Reference: (https://en.wikipedia.org/wiki/Shuttle_Training_Aircraft)

382.

North Korea issued a series of postage stamps featuring Prince Charles and Princess Diana. There were even celebrations in North Korea when the two were married.

Reference: (http://www.ibtimes.co.uk/princess-dianas-effect-north-korea-revealed-by-bizarre-postage-stamps-1634269)

383.

The country with the 3rd most English speakers is Pakistan.

Reference: (http://www.k-international.com/blog/countries-with-the-most-english-speakers/)

384.

In the 1850s, baseball had different rules in Massachusetts than it did in New York. Under the Massachusetts rules, you could throw the ball at a runner, and if you hit them, they were out.

Reference: (https://www.nytimes.com/2017/03/28/magazine/as-baseball-considers-change-it-should-look-to-its-past.html)

385.

In 1982, Kuwait's unofficial stock market had the 3rd highest market capitalization globally until it crashed due to high levels of speculation, unsecured post-dated cheques, and shell companies.

Reference: (https://en.wikipedia.org/wiki/Souk_Al-Manakh_stock_market_crash)

386.

Johns Hopkins University was founded by a Quaker.

Reference: (https://www.jhu.edu/about/history/)

387.

Alcohol breath is not from the stomach, rather it's from the ethanol diffusing out of the blood in the lungs. Eating food, chewing gum, or vomiting won't help mask how much alcohol is in your system if you're breathalyzed.

Reference: (https://sites.duke.edu/apep/module-4-alcohol-and-the-breathalyzer-test/content-ethanol-leaves-the-lungs-in-the-air/)

388.

German executioners wore top hat and bow ties at work.

Reference: (http://boisdejustice.com/Germany/Germany.html)

389.

Nigeria is the fourth largest English speaking country, behind the U.S., India and Pakistan.

Reference: (https://en.wikipedia.org/wiki/List_of_countries_by_English-speaking_population)

390.

Uber drivers in China changed their profile photos to ghosts and zombie images so that when potential passengers saw these pictures they would cancel the ride they'd just booked, thus earning the driver the cancellation fee.

Reference: (https://www.theguardian.com/technology/2016/sep/22/uber-ghost-drivers-zombie-profile-pictures)

391.

Since the introduction of the Tootsie Pop in 1931, the Indian on the wrapper has never been officially redeemable for free candy.

Reference: (https://www.snopes.com/fact-check/shooting-star/)

392.

"Lord of the Rings: Return of the King" won an Oscar for Best Original Song in 2003 with "Into the West".

Reference: (https://en.wikipedia.org/wiki/Into_the_West_(song)#Awards)

393.

A "mini-Olympics" event is held every 2 years between various tiny non-sovereign island communities known as the "Island Games".

Reference: (https://en.wikipedia.org/wiki/Island_Games)

394.

Giant pandas cannot detect umami because their umami taste receptors don't work properly. This means they can't taste meatiness, and don't show a preference for meat. Scientists believe this explains their strict bamboo diet, despite being closely related to other carnivores.

Reference: (https://www.ncbi.nlm.nih.gov/pubmed/20573776)

395.

Gibraltar has their own national basketball team.

Reference: (http://www.fiba.basketball/rankingmen)

396.

The "Rule of Six" is a study of queuing by University College London. It found that Brits queue for an average of 6 minutes before giving up, are reluctant to join a queue if it has more than 6 people in it and are comfortable with a minimum amount of 6 inches' space between other queuers.

Reference: (https://www.telegraph.co.uk/news/2017/02/16/rule-six-governs-long-queue-shop/)

397.

Fewer people have run a sub-four-minute mile than have climbed Mt. Everest.

Reference: (https://www.newyorker.com/news/sporting-scene/the-four-minute-man-forever)

398.

During the Kangi Famine, it was made legal for families to sell their children in hope of raising money to buy food, and also, grant their children a more fortunate household. This had the long-term effect of creating a significant servile class which remained for the next 400 years.

Reference: (https://en.wikipedia.org/wiki/Kangi#The_Kangi_Famine_(1229-1232))

399.

There are about 140 million Italians in the world but only about 60 million live in Italy.

Reference: (https://en.wikipedia.org/wiki/Italians)

400.

Chicago has a large pack of coyotes that patrol the city, hunting rats.

Reference: (https://www.npr.org/sections/krulwich/2010/12/08/131876027/60-wild-coyotes-patrol-chicago-and-occasionally-stop-at-convenience-stores)

401.

The German region of Saarland competed as a team separate from Germany, in the 1952 Olympics, as it was administered by France at the time and the Saarland locals did not want to join the French team.

Reference: (https://en.wikipedia.org/wiki/Saar_at_the_1952_Summer_Olympics)

402.

In 2015, we detected for the first time the merger of 2 black holes by measuring the gravitational waves emitted by the collision that happened 1.3 billion years ago.

Reference: (https://www.scientificamerican.com/article/gravitational-waves-discovered-from-colliding-black-holes1/)

403.

In 2017, musician Samir Mezrahi released “A a a a a Very Good Song”, which is 10 seconds of silence that, as its listed first alphabetically, will automatically be at the top of your iTunes playlist, purposefully giving you time to select a song you want to hear.

Reference: (https://www.independent.co.uk/life-style/gadgets-and-tech/news/itunes-download-chart-a-very-good-song-samir-mezrahi-iphone-apple-music-a7892286.html)

404.

The Government of Barbados issued a limited edition series of postage stamps featuring centenarians and super-centenarians, in 2016.

Reference: (https://mymodernmet.com/centenarians-of-barbados-stamps/)

405.

Ben Stiller originally wanted Keanu Reeves to play the part of Tugg Speedman in the movie “Tropic Thunder,” while wanting to cast himself as Tugg’s agent, Rick Peck.

Reference: (http://guyspeed.com/tropic-thunder-facts/?utm_source=zergnet.com&utm_medium=referral&utm_campaign=zergnet_66578)

406.

The accordion is widely taught in North Korea. It is known as the "national instrument" and North Korean students are expected to learn the accordion throughout their elementary and secondary education.

Reference: (https://en.wikipedia.org/wiki/Accordion#North_Korea)

407.

In the Latin American Spanish dubbing of the Star Wars films, the name R2-D2 is pronounced as "Arturito", or Little Arthur, which sounds similar to the English pronunciation.

Reference: (https://en.wikipedia.org/wiki/R2-D2)

408.

There’s a cavity in an altar by Shakespeare’s tomb.

Reference: (https://youtu.be/B-2AaElwQP0)

409.

Shortly before “Return of the Jedi”, Lucasfilm lost the original recording of the THX Deep Note. Because it was created by 20,000 lines of computer code, which then randomly spit out a new sound every time the program was run, it was only luck that they found it before the premier.

Reference: (https://www.fastcodesign.com/3027361/the-story-behind-the-thx-deep-note)

410.

The Street Fighter character Dee Jay's pants originally said "MANTIS" but since his right sprite is merely a mirror image of his left, the "N" and "S" would be reversed, so it was changed to "MAXIMUM".

Reference: (http://streetfighter.wikia.com/wiki/Dee_Jay)

411.

Feodor Vassilyev and his first wife hold the record for the most children a couple has parented, he also fathered 19 by his second wife, with a total of 69 children; sixteen pairs of twins, seven sets of triplets and four sets of quadruplets, between 1725 and 1765, in a total of 27 births.

Reference: (https://en.wikipedia.org/wiki/Feodor_Vassilyev)

412.

NASA considered using motorcycles on the Moon as a simpler alternative to the Lunar Rover.

Reference: (https://jalopnik.com/nasa-almost-sent-a-motorcycle-to-the-moon-1793535699)

413.

The child of Clark Gable and Loretta Young, Judy Lewis, had plastic surgery done on her ears to try to conceal the fact that she had her father's ears. She thought she was adopted until she was over 30.

Reference: (https://www.youtube.com/watch?v=uT68SySulXY&feature=youtu.be)

414.

Asbestos was used as a Christmas decoration in the 1940s.

Reference: (https://www.snopes.com/was-fake-snow-made-from-asbestos-marketed-as-christmas-decor/)

415.

More than 85% of residents of the United States believe they are less biased than the average American.

Reference: (https://en.wikipedia.org/wiki/Bias_blind_spot)

416.

Male kakapo parrots have a mating call that can be heard four miles away, but females can't tell where it's coming from.

Reference: (https://io9.gizmodo.com/5886679/this-is-the-worst-reproductive-strategy-in-the-animal-kingdom)

417.

On March 13th, 1943, a plot to kill Hitler by German army officers failed as a bomb planted aboard his plane failed to explode due to a faulty detonator.

Reference: (https://www.history.com/this-day-in-history/another-plot-to-kill-hitler-foiled)

418.

When you are anticipating sex, your hair grows faster.

Reference: (https://attireclub.org/2015/10/15/facts-about-hair/)

419.

Ex-BioWare developers were working on a Pirates of the Caribbean role playing game that was cancelled by Disney shortly after being revealed.

Reference: (https://www.youtube.com/watch?v=Thu-p-_usqw)

420.

For over 78 years, Oklahoma State Penitentiary's Annual Outlaw Rodeo in McAlester, Oklahoma has held the only "Behind the Walls" prison rodeo. Inmates are brought in from 10 prisons around the state to compete against each other and the animals.

Reference: (http://www.sharkonline.org/index.php/individual-rodeos/745-the-oklahoma-prison-rodeo)

421.

"Smog" is a combination of "smoke" and "fog" coined in 1905 by Dr. Henry Antoine Des Voeux to describe the possible airborne health risk in London.

Reference:(https://www.psi.ch/ceg/PublicationsEN/Piazzesi,_PhD_thesis,_ETH_Zurich,_2006.pdf)

422.

In 2015, more people died trying to take selfies than from shark attacks.

Reference: (https://www.usatoday.com/story/news/nation-now/2015/09/23/people-died-selfies-shark-attacks/72682068/)

423.

In 1994, a disgruntled FedEx employee tried to hijack and crash a cargo flight, using hammers and a spear gun. Despite serious injuries during the attack, the pilot and crew were able to land the plane. The pilot flew the DC-10 upside down at times in an attempt to stop the hijacker.

Reference: (https://en.wikipedia.org/wiki/Federal_Express_Flight_705)

424.

Shaquille O'Neill is the largest DJ and goes by the name DJ Diesel, also known as Shaq Fu.

Reference: (https://youtu.be/cgGjyK9JIB4)

425.

The word "Bridal" comes from the words "Bride-Ale", one of a series of beers brewed to celebrate special occasions. Some sources state that it just referred to the wedding feast or celebration but there are enough sources and references that there is a strong connection to brewing.

Reference: (https://beerandbrewing.com/dictionary/KgxDyNLIwN/bride-ale/)

426.

Since 1948, there has been a group of ladies at Arlington National Cemetery that has attended every funeral to support and comfort families, or to be there to ensure that no one is ever buried alone.

Reference: (https://www.aarp.org/home-family/friends-family/info-2016/arlington-ladies-military-grief.html)

427.

Henri Breault, a pediatrician in Ontario, Canada, was instrumental in the development of the child-safety cap for medicines. When introduced in the Windsor area in 1967, the design, known as the "Palm N Turn," quickly led to a 91% drop in accidental poisonings of children.

Reference: (http://www.cdnmedhall.org/inductees/dr-henri-j-breault)

428.

Lynyrd Skynyrd had to stop performing their song "Gimme Back My Bullets" due to fans taking it literally and throwing bullets and casings up on stage. The song was referring to song rating when talking about "bullets".

Reference: (http://www.gibson.com/news-lifestyle/features/en-us/10-things-lynyrd-skynyrd-1011-2012.aspx)

429.

Christopher Plummer, Martin Luther King Jr. and Anne Frank were born the same year, 1929.

Reference: (https://rayanworld.com/20180128121101002/Facts-That-Will-Shatter-Your-Perception-Of-Time?subarticle=13)

430.

The CIA measures the total miles of U.S. coastline at 18,924 miles while Congressional Research Institute puts it at 29,093 miles and NOAA at 95,471 miles; they are all correct thanks to the Coastline Paradox.

Reference: (https://www.youtube.com/watch?v=kFjq8PX6F7I)

431.

In 1983, a Rupert Murdoch owned newspaper was duped into publishing the faked diaries of Adolf Hitler.

Reference: (https://en.wikipedia.org/wiki/Hitler_Diaries)

432.

Under UN protocol, the President of the United States is to be addressed as "His Excellency."

Reference: (https://en.wikipedia.org/wiki/President_of_the_United_States)

433.

Gatorade used 2500 switches and motion capture technology to make animated water droplets appear as though it was people exercising.

Reference: (https://www.youtube.com/watch?time_continue=118&v=FG_1loacWoQ)

434.

Michael Buffer, the "Let's get ready to rumble" guy, had the phrase trademarked and as of 2009 it has generated $400 million dollars in revenue.

Reference: (https://en.wikipedia.org/wiki/Michael_Buffer#Trademark)

435.

D.B. Cooper is an unidentified man who hijacked a commercial plane in 1971. He demanded a $200,000 ransom and 4 parachutes. After his demands were met, he took the money and parachuted out of the plane. The FBI conducted a 45 year search but he still remains at large.

Reference: (https://en.wikipedia.org/wiki/D._B._Cooper)

436.

The expression, "blowing smoke (up your ass)", comes from a procedure thought to resuscitate drowning victims.

Reference: (https://gizmodo.com/blowing-smoke-up-your-ass-used-to-be-literal-1578620709)

437.

In 2011, an Amish family tried to ford a rain swollen creek in Kentucky, but the buggy flipped, killing four children.

Reference: (http://www.sandiegouniontribune.com/sdut-buggy-flips-in-ky-creek-killing-4-amish-children-2011feb26-story.html)

438.

The "historical fact" that the American government gave blankets infected with smallpox to Native Americans was made up by a single person.

Reference: (https://quod.lib.umich.edu/p/plag/5240451.0001.009/--did-the-us-army-distribute-smallpox-blankets-to-indians?rgn=main;view=fulltext)

439.

Metal Gear Solid 4 holds the world record for the longest cutscene in a video game at 71 minutes of uninterrupted cutscenes.

Reference: (http://www.houstonpress.com/arts/10-games-with-guinness-world-records-6392480)

440.

Saguaro National Park's cacti have microchip IDs implanted to prevent theft.

Reference: (http://www.nytimes.com/2008/10/12/us/12cactus.html)

441.

Target created an algorithm to detect which shoppers were in their second trimester of pregnancy. They sent baby marketing materials mixed in with lawn mowers and wine glasses so the women wouldn't suspect anything.

Reference:(http://www.slate.com/blogs/how_not_to_be_wrong/2014/06/09/big_data_what_s_even_creepier_than_target_guessing_that_you_re_pregnant.html)

442.

Norway gets 99% of its electric power from hydropower.

Reference: (https://en.wikipedia.org/wiki/Electricity_sector_in_Norway)

443.

Emotions can be "mapped" on the human body showing areas of somatosensory activation and deactivation for each emotion. The bodily topography for happiness and love are very similar.

Reference: (http://www.pnas.org/content/pnas/early/2013/12/26/1321664111.full.pdf)

444.

The U.S. has been using solar panels in space, on satellites, since 1958.

Reference: (https://en.wikipedia.org/wiki/Solar_panels_on_spacecraft#History)

445.

The adult website, PornHub, offered Boston a free snow plowing in March, 2017, but there is no evidence that they did the deed.

Reference: (https://www.bostonmagazine.com/news/2017/03/13/pornhub-snow-plow-boston/)

446.

During the Nepal Royal Massacre, the Crown Prince killed 10 family members and then himself. Conspiracies focus on the king's brother, since he was not in attendance, his wife and children were among the few survivors, and he was next in line for the throne after the king and two princes died.

Reference: (https://en.wikipedia.org/wiki/Nepalese_royal_massacre)

447.

74% of mothers and 70% of fathers reported preferential treatment toward one child.

Reference: (http://www.parents.com/toddlers-preschoolers/everything-kids/study-confirms-your-deepest-darkest-secret-you-do-have-a/)

448.

Mercury dissolves gold.

Reference: (https://www.youtube.com/watch?v=yAGYGGmUmUw)

449.

Food allergies are now 2 to 3 times higher compared to 1997. We have also seen diagnosed anaphylactic, life threatening, food reactions rise 377 percent from 2007 to 2016. As of 2011, one out of thirteen kids have a food allergy. To this day, scientists are still dumbfounded over this epidemic.

Reference: (https://www.nbcnews.com/news/amp/ncna805316)

450.

The Sentilese people in North Sentinel Island, a remote island part of the Andaman Islands of India, are believed to be direct descendants from the first humans who emerged from Africa, and have lived on the island for 60,000 years. They're extremely hostile and violent towards outsiders.

Reference: (https://www.youtube.com/watch?v=fEsNc1HXoYc&feature=youtu.be)

451.

In 1945, Vanderbilt University researchers knowingly fed pregnant women radioactive iron as part of a nutritional study. They used radioactive iron to more easily measure levels in blood and urine. The study resulted in one baby dying shortly after birth and three later developing childhood cancer.

Reference: (http://www.nytimes.com/1994/03/02/us/scientists-share-in-pain-of-experiment-debates.html?pagewanted=all)

452.

Lil'Wayne is 35 years old and has been active in the music business for 25 years.

Reference: (https://www.biography.com/people/lil-wayne-369134)

453.

Albert Einstein's brain was stolen by the pathologist performing the autopsy on his body.

Reference: (http://www.nationalgeographic.com.au/science/the-tragic-story-of-how-einsteins-brain-was-stolen-and-wasnt-even-special.aspx)

454.

The U.S. military fought German soldiers in Arizona during World War I in the Battle of Ambos Nogales.

Reference: (https://en.wikipedia.org/wiki/Battle_of_Ambos_Nogales)

455.

The U.S. military first fought German soldiers during the Revolutionary War and then again in the 2nd Samoan War before engaging in World War I and World War II against Germany.

Reference: (https://en.wikipedia.org/wiki/List_of_wars_involving_the_United_States)

456.

Mozart had a pet starling, which he bought after hearing him sing an excerpt from one of his pieces. After the starling died, Mozart wrote a humorous poem, which he read at its elaborate funeral.

Reference: (https://en.wikipedia.org/wiki/Mozart%27s_starling)

457.

During Stalin's time, the Soviet Union did not recognize Darwin's theory of evolution. Instead, they recognized Lysenkoism. It believed in heritability of acquired characteristics. For example, the state of being leafless as a result of having been plucked could be inherited by that organism's descendants.

Reference: (https://en.wikipedia.org/wiki/Lysenkoism)

458.

In 1962, researchers at the University of Oklahoma killed an elephant by overdosing it on LSD. They were attempting to induce "musth", which is elephant rage that occurs during mating season, so they injected a male elephant named Tusko with 297 milligrams of LSD. He fell over, defecated and died.

Reference: (https://www.theguardian.com/education/2002/aug/08/research.highereducation)

459.

In the 1930s, the Soviet Union attempted to domesticate wild moose. They believed moose might fare better in deep snow than horse cavalry, so they began a breeding program. Though they never became cavalry animals, one of the breeding facilities, Kostroma Moose Farm, is still up and running.

Reference: (https://en.wikipedia.org/wiki/Kostroma_Moose_Farm)

460.

The Liberal Democrat Party in the U.K. lost a parliamentary seat in 1994 because someone else stood for the seat under the name "Literal Democrat", causing enough people to vote for him in error to cause the Liberal Democrats to lose the seat.

Reference: (http://www.bbc.co.uk/news/av/uk-politics-27056001/bbc-rewind-a-literal-democrat)

461.

An anonymous Brit drew penises around potholes in Manchester to force authorities to stop delaying fixing them. It worked.

Reference: (https://www.theverge.com/2015/5/2/8535259/penis-pothole-activism-wanksy-england)

462.

William Walker MVO was an English diver famous for shoring up the southern and eastern sides of Winchester Cathedral.

Reference: (https://en.wikipedia.org/wiki/William_Walker_(diver))

463.

Only 10 percent of the child victimizers in violent crimes are strangers. Sex offences are the crimes least likely to involve strangers as perpetrators.

Reference: (https://en.wikipedia.org/wiki/Stranger_danger)

464.

There was a 5th Ice Age movie made in which one of the characters goes to space.

Reference: (https://youtu.be/Ohq6NmKMja8)

465.

Doctors are purposely tripping the elderly to make them more fall resistant. The therapy involves hooking them into a harness and having trainers shove, nudge and trip them off balance. The harness keeps them from falling and getting hurt while the exercises help train muscles for better balance.

Reference: (https://www.cbsnews.com/news/tripping-seniors-could-help-prevent-future-falls/)

466.

Daniel Burton was the first person to bicycle from the coast of Antarctica to the South Pole.

Reference: (http://archive.sltrib.com/article.php?id=57389591&itype=CMSID)

467.

In Florida, the blue light on top of traffic lights turns on when the signal is red, letting law enforcement know from obscure angles if a light is red, thus being able to better catch red light runners.

Reference: (https://www.wuft.org/news/2016/03/14/what-are-those-blue-lights-for-atop-traffic-signals/)

468.

The fake cocaine actor's snort on film is vitamin B powder, a common cutting agent for real cocaine.

Reference: (https://www.cinemablend.com/new/What-Actually-Fake-Cocaine-Actors-Snort-Movies-110187.html)

469.

The FBI tried to track suspected associates of Chilean leftists in the United States in the 1970's on behalf of Pinochet.

Reference: (http://www.nytimes.com/1999/02/10/world/fbi-helped-chile-search-for-leftists-files-show.html)

470.

Carole Hersee, the original girl who has been on multiple BBC's Test Cards since 1967, denied her Guinness World Record for the longest running TV appearance in 2007 because, "it isn't a record that somebody else can achieve, apparently."

Reference: (https://en.wikipedia.org/wiki/Carole_Hersee#References)

471.

The Great Wall of China is longer than Pluto.

Reference: (https://en.wikipedia.org/wiki/Orders_of_magnitude_(length)#Astronomical)

472.

The FBI monitored Gore Vidal for a decade after he mocked J. Edgar Hoover in his play "The Best Man".

Reference: (https://www.usnews.com/news/blogs/washington-whispers/2013/02/25/newly-public-fbi-document-shows-agency-kept-close-watch-on-gore-vidal)

473.

For a long time, the day in a leap year that was considered the extra day was not February 29th but rather February 24th.

Reference: (https://en.wikipedia.org/wiki/February_24)

474.

Experts believe that they've discovered the oldest sex toy in human history. The stone-like object is 28,000 years old and was found in a cave in the mountains of Germany. It measures eight inches long, three centimeters wide and would have likely also been used to help make tools by smashing rocks.

Reference: (http://www.huffingtonpost.co.uk/2015/01/19/stone-penis-28000-years-old_n_6499780.html)

475.

14 years prior to the sinking of the Titanic, an author named Morgan Robertson wrote "Wreck of the Titan, or Futility." The book is about an unsinkable ocean liner that strikes an iceberg and sinks in the Northern Atlantic.

Reference: (https://en.wikipedia.org/wiki/The_Wreck_of_the_Titan:_Or,_Futility#)

476.

King John of Bohemia, who was blind, died after leading a charge while tied to two other knights.

Reference: (https://en.wikipedia.org/wiki/John_of_Bohemia#Life)

477.

Kansas is flatter than a pancake.

Reference: (http://www.usu.edu/geo/geomorph/kansas.html)

478.

In 1929, Princeton researchers successfully turned a live cat into a functioning telephone.

Reference: (https://www.ripleys.com/weird-news/princeton-cat-experiment/)

479.

Dolly Parton's "Jolene" is about a red-headed clerk who had a crush on her husband, but the song is named after one of her fans. Dolly told her, "That is pretty. That sounds like a song. I'm going to write a song about that."

Reference: (https://www.npr.org/2008/10/09/95520570/dolly-partons-jolene-still-haunts-singers)

480.

A "purple unicorn" is a term used to describe someone who has characteristics that are considered rare and nearly impossible to find.

Reference: (http://www.unicornsrule.com/purple-unicorn/)

481.

Ball Lightning is a natural phenomenon produced during storms. It has been well documented, and it is typically described as a ball of electricity capable of passing through walls and other barriers. It was often believed to be ghost fires or apparitions in the olden days.

Reference: (https://www.scientificamerican.com/article/periodically-i-hear-stori/)

482.

"Orko" from "He–Man & the Masters of the Universe" was originally named "Gorpo". The cartoon company Filmation was so cheap that they changed his name to "Orko" so they could flip and reuse his animation cells more efficiently. Originally he had a big "G" on him that couldn't be reversed like an "O".

Reference: (http://he-man.wikia.com/wiki/Orko)

483.

SETI scientists believed that the chances for finding intelligent extraterrestrial life were far greater than initially expected, since Earth developed two intelligent species, humans and dolphins.

Reference: (https://www.space.com/12811-dolphin-intelligence-search-extraterrestrial-life.html)

484.

Scientists created an artificial womb and have successfully grown lamb fetuses.

Reference: (https://www.npr.org/sections/health-shots/2017/04/25/525044286/scientists-create-artificial-womb-that-could-help-prematurely-born-babies)

485.

A very deep earthquake with the epicenter on the South American country of Bolivia in 1994, was felt in a large area of the North American continent, with felt reports from Toronto, Minneapolis and Los Angeles.

Reference: (http://articles.latimes.com/1994-06-09/news/mn-2193_1_major-earthquake)

486.

15,152 forms of life have been found in the New York Subway system.

Reference: (http://time.com/3697797/new-york-city-subway-germs-bacteria-dna/)

487.

Joseph Pilates was a German working in England when World War I broke out. While interned in a prison camp, he developed a method of exercise prisoners could perform in confined space using just their own body weight. It worked well and was a hit, and he eventually moved to the U.S. in 1926.

Reference: (https://www.pilates.com/BBAPP/V/pilates/origins-of-pilates.html)

488.

Australians are the biggest bong users and pay the highest price for cocaine, according to the 2017 Global Drug Survey.

Reference: (https://www.smh.com.au/healthcare/global-drug-survey-2017-finds-australians-are-the-biggest-bong-users-pay-most-for-cocaine-20170523-gwb2jd.html)

489.

During the 1960s, Black Nationalist groups began pushing for the establishment of a country for black people in some portion of the current United States. They dubbed the country "The Republic of New Afrika".

Reference: (https://en.wikipedia.org/wiki/Republic_of_New_Afrika)

490.

Ice is considered a mineral.

Reference: (https://en.wikipedia.org/wiki/Ice)

491.

Richard McCoy Jr. was arrested for hijacking an airliner and is suspected of being the infamous D.B. Cooper.

Reference: (https://en.wikipedia.org/wiki/Richard_McCoy_Jr.)

492.

The Aquatic Ape Theory suggests that early hominids lived in water part of the time which accounts for our hairless bodies, our upright, two-legged walking and our layers of subcutaneous fat, which made us better insulated in water.

Reference: (https://en.wikipedia.org/wiki/Aquatic_ape_hypothesis)

493.

There exists a conspiracy theory which states that the government adds fluoride to our water for sinister reasons.

Reference:(http://www.slate.com/articles/health_and_science/science/2013/11/conspiracy_theory_psychology_people_who_claim_to_know_the_truth_about_jfk.html)

494.

When "Night of the Living Dead" was released in 1968 it was given an afternoon matinee, which meant a large portion of its audience was children.

Reference: (https://en.wikipedia.org/wiki/Night_of_the_Living_Dead#Release)

495.

In South Africa, and its neighbors, there's a custom called "lobola" or "bride price". The average payment is 10 cows or their equivalent cash value.

Reference: (https://www.iol.co.za/personal-finance/ways-to-save-for-lobola-10406762)

496.

Michele Amatore, or Quetto, was a black Sudanese slave who was taken to Italy and freed but enlisted in the Italian army and fought in all the Italian wars of independence earning the rank of captain in the elite unit of the Bersaglieri.

Reference: (https://en.wikipedia.org/wiki/Michele_Amatore)

497.

Armadillidiidae are crustaceans and have gills.

Reference: (https://www3.northern.edu/natsource/INVERT1/Pillbu1.htm)

498.

Due to the number of times a popular homeopathic remedy is "diluted," there would require to be 10 to the power 320 more universes to simply have one molecule of the original ingredient left in the final substance.

Reference: (https://en.wikipedia.org/wiki/Homeopathy)

499.

The Bible is the most stolen book in the world.

Reference: (http://money.cnn.com/gallery/pf/2013/06/07/bizarre-stolen-items/index.html)

500.

The Longines Symphonette was a pre-recorded classical music program that ran on the radio for 14 years.

Reference: (https://en.wikipedia.org/wiki/The_Longines_Symphonette)

501.

During the 1950's, artists such as Little Richard and Chuck Berry created rock'n'roll, but received little revenue and praise due to white artists creating socially acceptable covers of their songs.

Reference: (http://vcm.bc.ca/the-blanching-of-rock-and-roll/)

502.

The state of Wyoming has 2 escalators.

Reference: (https://www.npr.org/2013/07/18/203361119/where-are-all-of-wyomings-escalators)

503.

"Promaja" is a belief spread across the Balkans which states that you will get sick, get a headache, or pain in the bones if you leave windows in your house open so that it creates a draft.

Reference: (http://www.laura-dennis.com/the-dreaded-deadly-promaja/)

504.

Almost every kind of wild fish is infected with worms.

Reference: (https://munchies.vice.com/en_us/article/d755kx/almost-every-kind-of-wild-fish-is-infected-with-worms)

505.

Las Vegas's MGM Grand Hotel and Casino had its worst financial week ever when it hosted a physicist convention.

Reference: (http://physicsbuzz.physicscentral.com/2015/09/one-winning-move.html)

506.

North Korea's government is actually a necrocracy.

Reference: (http://www.asianews.it/news-en/Necrocracy-in-Pyongyang,-Kim-Jong-il-becomes-'grand-marshal'-23984.html)

507.

Swedish curse words are not bad enough, so Swedes borrow curses from English, German, and Finnish.

Reference: (https://en.wikipedia.org/wiki/Swedish_profanity)

508.

There's an amusement park in Hyderabad called Snow World which offers an indoor snow play area and snowfall to Indians who have never seen snow. Special warm jackets and water proof shoes are provided.

Reference: (http://snowworldhyd.com/gallary.html)

509.

Doug Jones from Guillermo Del Toro's Oscar-nominated "Shape of Water" was the first person to play McDonald's ad character Mac Tonight.

Reference: (https://en.wikipedia.org/wiki/Mac_Tonight)

510.

Munchausen by Internet is when individuals feign disease, illness, or psychological trauma to draw attention, sympathy, or reassurance to themselves. They seek attention by feigning illnesses in online venues such as chat rooms and message boards.

Reference: (https://en.wikipedia.org/wiki/Munchausen_by_Internet)

511.

Half a dozen actors in "To Kill a Mockingbird" also have appeared on "Star Trek".

Reference: (https://trekkerscrapbook.com/2015/07/15/hey-that-guy-was-on-star-trek-to-kill-a-mockingbird-1963/)

512.

The Soviet Luna 3 Moon probe used film taken from captured U.S. surveillance balloons due to the fact that they couldn't manufacture radiation-hardened film yet.

Reference: (https://www.diyphotography.net/the-weird-story-of-the-us-sending-camera-coffins-to-space-and-the-soviets-repurposing-them-into-moon-fax-cameras/)

513.

Kirk Kerkorian, the richest person in Los Angeles, has given more than $200 million and a school, and he has never allowed anything to be named in his honor.

Reference: (https://en.wikipedia.org/wiki/Kirk_Kerkorian)

514.

English words like "matter" and "material" come from the Latin word mater, meaning mother, since they believed all things and organisms were spontaneously generated by "Mother Earth."

Reference: (https://en.wikipedia.org/wiki/Three-age_system#The_Progress_of_Lucretius)

515.

Nickelodeon aired a kid's puppet show named "Weinerville" from July, 1993, to June, 1994.

Reference: (https://en.wikipedia.org/wiki/Weinerville)

516.

Alan Magee is an American airman who survived a fall from 22,000 feet, 6,700 meter, by fortuitously breaking through the glass roof of a railroad station near impact.

Reference: (https://en.wikipedia.org/wiki/Alan_Magee)

517.

The first two women to climb the Matterhorn did so in skirts and the third, Annie Smith Peck, was nearly arrested as she was the first to do so in pants.

Reference: (https://www.adventure-journal.com/2014/11/historical-badass-annie-smith-peck/)

518.

During the Great Leap Forward in China, communal agriculture began with taxation based on harvest yields. Commune officials artificially inflated yields to gain merit. The state eventually took most of the harvest which resulted in an estimated 30 million Chinese starving to death.

Reference: (https://www.youtube.com/watch?v=PJyoX_vrlns&feature=youtu.be&t=2340)

519.

The actor who was inside R2-D2 hated the guy who played C-3PO, calling him, "the rudest man I've ever met."

Reference: (https://nypost.com/2015/12/13/he-might-as-well-be-a-bucket-why-c3po-and-r2d2-hate-each-other/)

520.

Fred Rogers is credited with the continued funding of PBS after he presented a passionate argument in front of the U.S. Senate in May, 1969. This allowed healthy child development shows like “Mr. Rogers Neighborhood” to be fully funded, along with the rest of PBS programming.

Reference: (http://www.businessinsider.com/mister-rogers-1969-defense-pbs-2012-10)

521.

Soap nuts contain saponin and we can wash our hands by wiping them between wet palms. As it releases a natural detergent it is even possible to wash clothes with these nuts.

Reference: (https://www.youtube.com/watch?v=WL4wgCeON2Q)

522.

80% of businesses in Sicily, Italy pay a protection fee to the Mafia.

Reference: (https://en.wikipedia.org/wiki/Pizzo_(extortion)#cite_note-tel241007-5)

523.

In China, dragons are not monsters but wise and benevolent creatures, which is why they were, and still are, associated with rulers.

Reference: (https://www.ancient.eu/article/1125/the-dragon-in-ancient-china/)

524.

In 1881, the Isle of Man became the first nation in the world to give women the right to vote.

Reference: (http://www.tynwald.org.im/education/women/Pages/VotesForWomen.aspx)

525.

British TV show "The Mighty Boosh" has won the NME Awards Best TV Show for three consecutive years, even though no new episodes were released after they won for the first year.

Reference: (https://en.wikipedia.org/wiki/The_Mighty_Boosh#Awards)

526.

In the late 1990's, NASA was researching the possibility of landing the shuttle boosters with oblique wings.

Reference: (https://ntrs.nasa.gov/archive/nasa/casi.ntrs.nasa.gov/20020023962.pdf)

527.

Hip-Hop group The Coup had an album called "Party Music." The album cover had to be changed because it showed them blowing up the World Trade Center. The cover was only made months before 9/11.

Reference: (https://www.wired.com/2001/09/eerie-image-pulled-from-cd/)

528.

There is a Mickey Mouse shaped solar farm at Disney World, Florida.

Reference: (https://ohmy.disney.com/news/2016/04/14/mickey-shaped-solar-facility-activated-near-walt-disney-world/)

529.

Donald Lau, who has been Chief Fortune Cookie Writer at Wonton Foods for over 30 years, is retiring due to writer's block.

Reference: (https://nypost.com/2017/02/14/fortune-cookie-writer-of-30-years-quitting-over-writers-block/)

530.

David Faustino, the actor who played Bud Bundy in "Married with Children," was a rapper.

Reference: (https://www.youtube.com/watch?v=2AaQDK0tpt8)

531.

The recipient of Nicholas Green's heart lived a previously unimaginable normal life for 22 years before eventually dying of respiratory failure.

Reference: (http://www.latimes.com/opinion/op-ed/la-oe-green-death-of-recipient-of-nicholas-greens-heart-20170210-story.html)

532.

The Rubik's Cube is the bestselling toy in the world, selling 350 million units since 1980.

Reference: (https://www.usatoday.com/story/money/business/2014/05/18/24-7-wall-st-the-best-selling-products-of-all-time/9223465/)

533.

According to current models, it takes a photon about 170,000 years to make it three quarters the way out of the Sun, starting at the core.

Reference: (https://www.reddit.com/user/momscooking)

534.

Out of the 4 to 5 thousand mammal species, female humans are the only ones whose breasts remain permanently enlarged when not lactating.

Reference: (https://www.theguardian.com/science/2010/may/14/breast-size-evolution)

535.

In June 2017, a tire shop in Fort Worth, Texas, was robbed so often that the owner bought a guard dog. The next time the shop was robbed, the intruders stole the dog.

Reference: (https://www.dallasnews.com/news/fort-worth/2017/06/12/guard-dog-stolen-often-robbed-fort-worth-tire-shop)

536.

Einstein the Parrot gave a TED talk and does dozens of impressions on cue.

Reference:(http://www.slate.com/articles/video/video/2017/04/watch_einstein_the_parrot_do_hilarious_impressions_video.html?wpsrc=sh_all_mob_tw_top)

537.

There are 35 glaciers in Africa. They are all located in East Africa, in the Ruwenzori Range and other volcanic summits.

Reference: (https://en.wikipedia.org/wiki/List_of_glaciers_in_Africa)

538.

The penguin, as an animal, seems to be made up of an equal proportion of a mammal, fish, and fowl. It tastes like a piece of beef, an odoriferous codfish, and a canvas-back duck, roasted in a pot, with blood and cod-liver oil for sauce.

Reference: (http://www.south-pole.com/p0000083.htm)

539.

Bacteria in urine of some patients with urinary catheters produce an enzyme, indoxyl phosphatase, which turns urine purple.

Reference: (https://en.wikipedia.org/wiki/Purple_urine_bag_syndrome)

540.

We have no idea why London is actually called London.

Reference:(http://archive.museumoflondon.org.uk/MuseumOfLondon/Templates/microsites/londinium/article.aspx?NRMODE=Published&NRNODEGUID=%7B43F5954B-D51C-4FAF-AF8D-63644DECA2D6%7D&NRORIGINALURL=%2FLondinium%2Fanalysis%2Fpubliclife%2Fadministration%2F4%2BLondin.htm&NRCACHEHINT=NoModifyGuestt)

541.

Phil Collins donated the world's largest private collection of Alamo artifacts to the state of Texas. It included a fringed leather pouch and a gun used by Davy Crockett and Jim Bowie's legendary knife.

Reference: (https://www.cbsnews.com/news/phil-collins-hands-over-alamo-collection-to-texas/)

542.

Rhode Island has the highest percentage of Italian-Americans in the U.S. at 18.9% while Arkansas has the lowest percentage at 1.6%.

Reference: (https://en.wikipedia.org/wiki/Italian_Americans#Demographics)

543.

Patrick Stewart voiced the Poop emoji in The Emoji Movie.

Reference: (https://www.usatoday.com/story/life/entertainthis/2017/07/29/patrick-stewart-talking-poop-emoji-most-non-poopy-thing-the-emoji-movie/522197001/)

544.

The turntable in your microwave switches directions every time it's used so that it can rotate a heavier load.

Reference: (http://www.nytimes.com/2013/04/16/science/why-does-my-microwaves-turntable-switch-directions.html)

545.

Road damage mostly results from trucks and buses. The damage a vehicle causes is proportional to the axle load raised to the fourth power, so doubling the weight an axle carries actually causes 16 times as much damage.

Reference: (https://en.wikipedia.org/wiki/Asphalt_concrete#Degradation_and_restoration)

546.

There is a hexagonal hurricane on Saturn.

Reference: (https://en.wikipedia.org/wiki/Saturn%27s_hexagon)

547.

The full Moon in March is called the Worm Moon because the earthworm casts are seen in the ground as the ground thaws.

Reference: (https://moon.nasa.gov/news/43/moon-missive-the-next-full-moon-is-the-worm-moon-crow-moon-crust-moon-sap-moon-sugar-moon-or-lenten-m/)

548.

A Canadian man named ManWoman tried to reclaim the swastika as a symbol of good luck and prosperity.

Reference: (https://www.vice.com/en_us/article/avn78e/manwoman-is-taking-back-the-swastika)

549.

Musician Mike Edwards, who was an original member of the band ELO, was killed when a cylindrical bale of hay rolled down a hill and crashed into the van he was driving.

Reference: (https://en.wikipedia.org/wiki/Mike_Edwards_(musician)#Death)

550.

The Mad River Glen ski area is one of the only two ski areas in the U.S. that operates a single-chair ski lift.

Reference: (https://en.wikipedia.org/wiki/Mad_River_Glen#Single_Chair)

551.

A man worked at the restaurant at the top of the World Trade Center. After 9/11, they never saw him again and presumed he died in the towers. In 2003, the government removed his name from the 9/11 memorial as he might have used the tragedy to start a new life without telling his family.

Reference: (https://melmagazine.com/arturo-alva-moreno-was-9-11-victim-2-754-or-was-he-987ab8e4a6f0?gi=5d9d871355b1)

552.

PagPags are food scraps sold as a staple for the Philippine's poor.

Reference: (https://edition.cnn.com/2012/04/30/world/asia/philippines-pagpag-slums/index.html)

553.

According to “The World Factbook”, Norway has the second longest coastline in the world, despite being only the 68th largest country by area.

Reference: (https://en.wikipedia.org/wiki/List_of_countries_by_length_of_coastline)

554.

There is a "glut" of pet parrots in the U.S. due to them outliving humans.

Reference: (https://www.petmd.com/bird/care/how-long-do-birds-live)

555.

The production of Def Leppard's album "Hysteria" was so expensive that guitarist Phil Collen estimated they needed to sell around 5 million copies to break even. They ended up selling 25 million.

Reference: (https://en.wikipedia.org/wiki/Hysteria_(Def_Leppard_album)#History)

556.

The Tacoma Narrows Bridge was built failing to account for certain wind effects. The suspension bridge would only last 4 months before a spectacular collapse.

Reference: (https://www.youtube.com/watch?v=j-zczJXSxnw)

557.

In 1979, there was an unexplainable nuclear explosion near the Prince Edward Islands. It was detected by the Vela Hotel Satellite, but still has yet to be claimed.

Reference: (https://en.wikipedia.org/wiki/Vela_Incident)

558.

Thomas Jefferson once dislocated his wrist while trying to impress a woman that he liked.

Reference: (https://www.monticello.org/site/research-and-collections/wrist-injury-1786)

559.

One of the original album cover design ideas for Led Zeppelin's "Houses of the Holy" was to sneakily bulldoze out the "Zoso" logo among the Nazca lines in Peru and photograph it from a helicopter.

Reference: (https://www.rollingstone.com/music/lists/hipgnosis-album-covers-from-pink-floyd-to-led-zeppelin-w475109/led-zeppelin-houses-of-the-holy-1973-w475113)

560.

From late June, 2017, onwards, tens of women in various states of India and Nepal had their hair mysteriously chopped off, and no one yet knows how, why, or who did it.

Reference: (https://en.wikipedia.org/wiki/Hair_chopping_incidents_in_South_Asia)

561.

Top-level football stadiums in the United Kingdom are banned from having standing-room only sections due to the 1989 Hillsborough disaster.

Reference: (https://www.theguardian.com/football/2014/feb/13/premier-league-standing-ban-stadiums-football-league-aston-villa-rail-seat)

562.

The Boston Bruins climbed over the glass at Madison Square Garden to beat up unruly Rangers fans.

Reference: (https://www.youtube.com/watch?v=VMcbdBYuGTE&feature=youtu.be&t=1m32s)

563.

The battlecruiser SMS Seydlitz sank three times. The third time was because the man in charge wasn't there when it was raised, so he made them re-sink it so he could get the photo-op.

Reference: (https://en.wikipedia.org/wiki/SMS_Seydlitz)

564.

Airplane pilots actually increase power to the engines when landing to help the plane slow down. This is because of the reverse thrusters on the engine.

Reference: (https://www.youtube.com/watch?v=cfFZ2-Am-Zk&feature=youtu.be)

565.

Manuka honey can be used as part of wound dressing to facilitate wound recovery.

Reference: (https://www.advancedtissue.com/honey-can-help-wound-healing/)

566.

Ubisoft partnered with a British Museum to apply machine learning to speed the deciphering of ancient hieroglyphics.

Reference: (https://hieroglyphicsinitiative.ubisoft.com/en-GB/home)

567.

A U.S. President can serve in office for 10 years in special circumstances.

Reference: (https://constitutioncenter.org/interactive-constitution/amendments/amendment-xxii)

568.

An 18-month-old German shepherd named Luna fell off a boat in the Pacific Ocean, swam 2 miles to a nearby island, and survived for 5 weeks by eating mice before she was rescued by a team of Navy staffers. She was found to be slightly under-nourished, but in perfect condition otherwise.

Reference: (http://abcnews.go.com/US/navy-finds-missing-dog-fell-off-fishing-boat/story?id=37701943)

569.

Alexander Hamilton was only 19 or 21 years old when the American Revolution began in 1776.

Reference: (http://wikipedia.org/wiki/Alexander_Hamilton)

570.

The U.S. Army does not keep any record of "confirmed kills". Servicemen routinely report successful hits to their superiors and personally keep track.

Reference: (https://www.nbcnews.com/news/other/confirmed-kills-solemn-secret-military-snipers-becoming-pop-culture-hit-f6C10791983)

571.

It takes 1,700 liters, or 450 gallons, of water to make the typical 100 gram, or 3.5 ounce, chocolate bar. Growing of the actual cocoa plant uses up the majority of this water.

Reference: (https://blog.nationalgeographic.org/2015/02/12/love-water-for-chocolate/)

572.

For several years, Coca-Cola has been making a kosher Coke product for Passover.

Reference: (https://newrepublic.com/article/112747/112747)

573.

There are U.S. presidential pet hamsters named Debbie and Billie. Billie ate his own children, who was then eaten by Debbie, who then died of indigestion.

Reference: (http://www.presidentialpetmuseum.com/pets/jfk-hamsters-debbie-billie/)

574.

Oxford University Professor Sir Andrew Wiles was awarded the Abel Prize and $700,000 in 2016 for solving a 358-year-old math problem known as "Fermat's Last Theorem." Fermat himself claimed to have found proof for the theorem, but the margins of his notes weren't wide enough to contain it.

Reference: (http://www.ox.ac.uk/news/2016-03-15-fermats-last-theorem-proof-secures-mathematics-top-prize-sir-andrew-wiles)

575.

The practice of Sati, where a Hindu wife immolates herself on her husband's pyre, has been banned in India since 1829. This practice is now rare but does occur in rural areas in India.

Reference: (https://www.theguardian.com/world/2008/oct/14/india)

576.

San Diego's frozen zoo, which houses over 10,000 living cell cultures, oocytes, sperm, and embryos, is one of less than a dozen frozen zoos in the world.

Reference: (http://institute.sandiegozoo.org/resources/frozen-zoo)

577.

Scientists didn't know where birds went in the winter until 1822. That year, a stork was seen in Germany with an arrow from central Africa lodged in its neck, having flown 3,000 kilometers in its wounded state. This provided the final proof that birds migrate.

Reference: (https://www.atlasobscura.com/places/zoological-collection-of-the-university-of-rostock#)

578.

Licorice is mildly poisonous and should not be eaten during pregnancy or in quantities exceeding 70 to 150 grams per day.

Reference: (https://en.wikipedia.org/wiki/Liquorice#Licorice_poisoning)

579.

The color orange was named after the fruit.

Reference: (https://en.wikipedia.org/wiki/Orange_(colour)#Etymology)

580.

A Black Hole was caught swallowing a star that got too close. Some of the stellar debris fell into the Black Hole and some of it was ejected into space at high speeds.

Reference: (https://www.nasa.gov/mission_pages/galex/galex20120502.html)

581.

Benedict Arnold was in fact an American war hero who, due to his actions at Saratoga, helped America win the revolution.

Reference: (http://www.history.com/topics/american-revolution/benedict-arnold)

582.

Between 1999 and 2014, the suicide rate in the United States increased by 24%.

Reference: (https://en.wikipedia.org/wiki/Suicide_in_the_United_States)

583.

In 1964, a man in Cologne, Germany attacked a school with a homemade flamethrower, a lance made from a broomstick, and a mace, killing 10 and injuring 22.

Reference: (https://en.wikipedia.org/wiki/Cologne_school_massacre)

584.

“For He's a Jolly Good Fellow” has different lyrics in England and America.

Reference: (https://en.wikipedia.org/wiki/For_He%27s_a_Jolly_Good_Fellow)

585.

There is an NGO in Bangladesh that sells 10,000 meals daily at only 1 Taka, or 0.012 USD, per meal instead of giving it for free, so people don't feel like they are begging.

Reference: (http://bidyanondo.org/all-project-list/one-tk-meal/)

586.

Since 2006, Rovaniemi in northern Finland has been the largest city in the European Union by area at 8,016.75 square kilometers.

Reference: (https://en.wikipedia.org/wiki/Rovaniemi)

587.

You will never see a bin being emptied in Disneyland because of a series of hidden tunnels.

Reference: (https://www.thescottishsun.co.uk/news/1522611/15-secrets-you-didnt-know-about-disney-theme-parks/)

588.

A device exists, and was approved by the FDA in 2015, that allows blind people to see with their tongue.

Reference: (https://www.scientificamerican.com/article/device-lets-blind-see-with-tongues/)

589.

The reason NBA player Elfrid Payton hasn't cut his hair since 2011 is because he vowed not to do so until his old high school team wins a state championship.

Reference: (https://en.wikipedia.org/wiki/Elfrid_Payton_(basketball))

590.

There is an Aboriginal story where the Moon's penis becomes detached from his body and slithers, "like a snake in the grass", after his seven daughters before making love to the oldest.

Reference: (http://www.kitezh.com/sevensisters/7sisters.htm)

591.

The CVS in CVS Pharmacy stands for Consumer Value Store and didn't have a pharmacy department in most of their stores until three years after the chain's opening in 1964.

Reference: (https://en.wikipedia.org/wiki/CVS_Pharmacy)

592.

Originally built as only a hunting lodge for King Francois I, Chateau de Chambord contains 440 rooms and 365 fireplaces. It is so large that the Loire was rumored to be diverted to make room.

Reference: (https://wanderwisdom.com/travel-destinations/Castles-in-France)

593.

Scrotox is the process of injecting Botox into the testicles to improve the cosmetic look of a man's genitals.

Reference: (https://tonic.vice.com/en_us/article/599xdx/i-botoxed-my-balls-to-make-them-look-nicer)

594.

George Washington had Taphephobia, which the fear of being buried alive. He was adamant about being put into the morgue 3 days after his death to make sure he wasn't "accidentally" alive.

Reference: (http://mentalfloss.com/article/64180/10-famous-people-who-were-afraid-theyd-be-buried-alive)

595.

The creator of the Carolina Reaper, the hottest pepper in the world, claims to have unreleased peppers that are more than twice as hot.

Reference: (https://www.youtube.com/watch?v=hrF3jVppfr4&feature=youtu.be&t=2m38s)

596.

When he realized he left a Trilby hat at home, Bono paid £1,000 to have it flown to Italy, occupying its own first-class seat. The crew feared that it might be damaged so they stored it in the cockpit alongside the captain.

Reference: (https://www.telegraph.co.uk/comment/personal-view/3634411/Profile-Bono.html)

597.

As recently as 1950, around 3.5 million U.S. farms kept dairy cows; by 2012, that number had dwindled to 58,000.

Reference: (https://modernfarmer.com/2017/05/explainer-trumps-milk-war-canada/)

598.

Los Angeles has its very own 44-story Twin Towers designed by original the original World Trade Center architect Minoru Yamasaki. They were even opened just two years after the much taller New York City towers.

Reference: (https://en.wikipedia.org/wiki/Century_Plaza_Towers)

599.

On the Scottish Isle of Rhum, the red deer population decapitate small bird chicks and eat the skulls for minerals like calcium. The deer have adapted this behavior because the island's vegetation lacks the key minerals.

Reference: (https://asknature.org/strategy/diet-compensates-for-mineral-deficiencies/#.WpoDtyJOmEc)

600.

In 1957, Argentine F1 driver Juan Manuel Fangio broke the lap time record at the German Grand Prix 10 times in one race. In 22 laps, he broke the standing record then beat his own record 9 more times. After making up a 48 second deficit he passed the leader on the last lap to take the win.

Reference: (https://en.wikipedia.org/wiki/Maserati_250F)

601.

NVidia's new AI can create eerily realistic traffic cam videos, changing winter to summer and sunshine to rain.

Reference: (https://thenextweb.com/artificial-intelligence/2017/12/04/nvidias-new-ai-creates-disturbingly-convincing-fake-videos/)

602.

Ethiopia adopted Christianity as its main religion before the Roman Empire did, the former happening in 330AD versus 380AD for the latter.

Reference: (https://en.wikipedia.org/wiki/Christianity_in_Ethiopia#Christian_Roots)

603.

The Caterpillar Club consists solely of people who have jumped out of a failing airplane and survived by deploying their parachute. The club was founded by Leslie Irvin, who survived ejecting out of his plane in 1919, and every member is sent a gold caterpillar pin with amethyst eyes.

Reference: (http://www.militaryhistoryonline.com/general/articles/caterpillarclub.aspx)

604.

Disco Demolition Night in 1979 at Comiskey Park is considered by many to be the death date of the Disco genre. A crate filled with disco records was blown up and thousands of fans stormed the field united in their hate of Disco.

Reference: (https://www.youtube.com/watch?v=I1CP1751wJA)

605.

Subutai carried out more than 20 campaigns in which he conquered 32 countries, won 65 pitched battles and conquered more territory than any other commander in history.

Reference: (https://en.wikipedia.org/wiki/Subutai)

606.

The mascot of the Arkansas School for the Deaf is the leopard. It wasn't chosen because of the band Def Leppard, but the band has met the football team.

Reference: (http://www.businessinsider.com/ap-def-leppard-meets-arkansas-school-for-the-deaf-leopards-2016-5)

607.

Pearl Jam was originally called "Mookie Blaylock", after the then-active NBA player of the same name; his jersey number was "10".

Reference: (http://www.twofeetthick.com/2011/03/10/how-did-mookie-blaylock-become-pearl-jam/)

608.

Vesna Vulović fell 33,330 feet out of an exploding plane and survived.

Reference: (https://en.wikipedia.org/wiki/Vesna_Vulovi%C4%87)

609.

The United States Air Force Pararescue use the sound bite of "Leeroy Jenkins" from World of Warcraft to notify themselves of an upcoming medevac mission.

Reference: (https://en.wikipedia.org/wiki/Leeroy_Jenkins)

610.

Between 1,000 and 4,000 people live in Antarctica at any given time. They are researchers and tourists. No permanent residents exist in Antarctica.

Reference: (https://www.interestinganswers.com/government/how-many-people-live-antarctica/)

611.

Resuci Anne's body was found drifting in a river in Paris; the mortician presented her face mask. People saw her beauty and made molds of the mask. Copies traveled across Europe and made it a hit decoration. When a toymaker created the first CPR dummies, he needed a face and Anne's was chosen.

Reference: (https://www.medelita.com/blog/from-suicide-to-cpr-the-origin-of-resusci-anne/)

612.

In the metric and SI unit system, all units are in lowercase, except for those that are named after someone.

Reference: (https://en.wikipedia.org/wiki/SI_base_unit)

613.

Contrary to popular belief, canes aren't meant to be used on the same side as your injury. While it seems logical to want to support the injured leg, you are actually meant to walk with the cane opposite your bad leg as to lean your weight away from the injury, rather than against the bad leg.

Reference: (https://www.youtube.com/watch?v=R0r6a8AE6Xw)

614.

The voting age in Italy depends on the office; the minimum voting age for the Chamber of Deputies is 18, but only those who are 25 or older can vote for the Senate.

Reference: (https://en.wikipedia.org/wiki/Italian_Parliament)

615.

The world's tallest man saved two dolphins by using his long arms to reach into them and pull out plastic they had ingested.

Reference: (http://news.bbc.co.uk/2/hi/asia-pacific/6178659.stm)

616.

To prepare Colin Farrell for his role in "Miami Vice," two undercover agents had the actor join them on a botched drug deal and only told him it was fake after the actor was showing signs of severe stress.

Reference: (https://www.youtube.com/watch?v=wsVIRHakog8&t=4m11s)

617.

Velociraptors were, in reality, only the size of a common turkey. They were probably feathered like one, too.

Reference: (https://wikipedia.org/wiki/Velociraptor?wprov=sfla1)

618.

The rapper Drake visited Drake University in the middle of the night after students gave up trying to get him to visit during a tour stop.

Reference: (http://college.usatoday.com/2016/10/06/that-time-drake-made-a-surprise-visit-to-drake-university/)

619.

Almost two-thirds of both houses of the U.S. Congress voted to outlaw school segregation in the U.S. in 1874.

Reference:(https://chicagounbound.uchicago.edu/cgi/viewcontent.cgi?article=12612&context=journal_articles)

620.

From 1925 to 1969, there was a Wrigley Field in Los Angeles. Baseball was played there for 33 season spanning from 1925 to 1957.

Reference: (https://en.wikipedia.org/wiki/Wrigley_Field_(Los_Angeles))

621.

In some areas, laundry detergent has become such a hot commodity item, that criminals steal it from stores to resell. Police call the detergent "liquid gold" on the black market and it's been known to be traded or sold for illegal drugs.

Reference: (https://en.wikipedia.org/wiki/Tide_(brand)#History)

622.

Using one's middle name initials enhances other's evaluations of their intellectual performance.

Reference: (https://ulir.ul.ie/bitstream/handle/10344/5412/Igou_2014_middle.pdf)

623.

Winston Churchill predicted the invention and rise of lab grown meat over 80 years ago. He stated, "We shall escape the absurdity of growing a whole chicken in order to eat the breast or wing, by growing these parts separately under a suitable medium."

Reference: (https://www.reuters.com/article/us-shapiro-meat-commentary/commentary-science-fiction-no-more-can-lab-grown-meat-feed-and-save-the-world-idUSKCN1GA25H)

624.

The New York Yankees uniform does not feature a name on the back. This is due to the club believing that putting the names on the back puts unneeded attention on the players, rather than the team as a whole.

Reference: (http://www.banderasnews.com/1010/nw-nyyankees.htm)

625.

Some people can raise their goosebumps at will.

Reference: (https://peerj.com/preprints/26594/)

626.

A "steep learning curve" does not mean an activity is difficult to learn. It means the opposite: rapid progress is made over time.

Reference: (https://en.wikipedia.org/wiki/Learning_curve)

627.

There is only one deaf dentist in Egypt.

Reference: (http://www.bbc.co.uk/news/av/disability-39566586/the-woman-who-fought-to-become-egypt-s-only-deaf-dentist)

628.

The guy that played the ferry captain in “Sully” was the actual ferry captain that first came to rescue passengers.

Reference: (http://www.myveronanj.com/2016/09/19/vincent-lombardi-plays-sully/)

629.

Abercrombie & Fitch's store on Madison Avenue in New York City used to sell guns and had a shooting range in its basement.

Reference: (https://www.bloomberg.com/news/articles/2017-10-19/abercrombie-fitch-puts-its-clothes-back-on)

630.

The classic opening guitar riff of "Johnny B. Goode" is actually a note-for-note copy of the opening of Louis Jordan's "Ain't That Just Like a Woman".

Reference: (https://en.wikipedia.org/wiki/Johnny_B._Goode)

631.

All of America's trash for the next 1,000 years would fit in a 35 by 35 mile landfill with a height of just 200 feet.

Reference: (https://youtu.be/Ms1lN-OJ6Ko)

632.

Out of the fourteen 8,000 meter peaks, Annapurna is the most dangerous to climb with an expedition fatality to successful ascent ratio of 38%.

Reference: (https://skyaboveus.com/climbing-hiking/annapurna-circuit)

633.

During the Aversion Project, nearly 1,000 patients were submitted to chemical castrations and electric shock treatment that was meant to "cure" them of their homosexual "condition."

Reference: (https://en.wikipedia.org/wiki/The_Aversion_Project)

634.

After surviving the plane crash that killed three of his bandmates, Artimus Plyle, the drummer of Lynyrd Skynyrd, was shot in the shoulder by a farmer as he stumbled through a field with a group of survivors.

Reference: (https://en.wikipedia.org/wiki/Artimus_Pyle#Lynyrd_Skynyrd)

635.

Emile Griffith beat Benny Paret in a fight that led to Paret's death. During the weigh-in, Paret mocked Griffith by grabbing Griffith's buttock and the used a Spanish homosexual slur. Griffith later came bisexual.

Reference: (https://www.newyorker.com/culture/culture-desk/death-at-the-garden)

636.

The famous stretch of road in San Francisco called the Embarcadero used to be covered by a double decker freeway until it was damaged in the 1988 earthquake.

Reference: (https://en.wikipedia.org/wiki/California_State_Route_480)

637.

Thales of Miletus was a pre-Socratic individual credited with being the first philosopher ever, the first person to accurately predict a solar eclipse, and the first person in history to receive credit for a mathematical discovery.

Reference: (https://en.wikipedia.org/wiki/Thales_of_Miletus)

638.

Tennis balls can be either "pressurized" or "pressureless". There are subtle differences, but it's possible the pressureless ones can contribute to strain injuries because they're a bit heavier. Pressurized ones start off bouncier, but go flat in a matter of days.

Reference: (http://tennisfixation.com/whats-difference-between-pressurized.html)

639.

7 of the top 10 most densely populated towns in America are in New Jersey.

Reference:(https://en.wikipedia.org/wiki/List_of_United_States_cities_by_population_density#Census-designated_places)

640.

The first attempt to invade Cuba from the U.S. was in 1849 by Narciso Lopez.

Reference: (https://en.wikipedia.org/wiki/Narciso_L%C3%B3pez#Career_as_a_filibuster)

641.

The Jackson 5 received only 2.8% royalties from Motown, so they signed with Epic for 20%. After being sued for breach of contract, Motown allowed the group to leave, as long as they changed their name, since "Jackson 5" was owned by Motown. The brothers renamed themselves simply "The Jacksons."

Reference: (https://en.wikipedia.org/wiki/The_Jackson_5#Decline_and_exit)

642.

In 1920, The New York Times ridiculed Robert H. Goddard and claimed that rockets could not function in space. On July 17, 1969, a day after the Apollo 11 launch, New York Times formally acknowledged their error.

Reference: (https://www.popsci.com/military-aviation-amp-space/article/2009-07/new-york-times-nasa-youre-right-rockets-do-work-space)

643.

The Guns N' Roses song, "November Rain," was being worked on as early as 1983 by Axl Rose. It wasn't released until 1991 when it was included on the "Use Your Illusion I" album, which released the same day as "Use Your Illusion II."

Reference: (https://uproxx.com/music/guns-n-roses-rare-facts/5/)

644.

During World War I, Britain manufactured thousands of tanks while Germany only made 20.

Reference: (https://en.wikipedia.org/wiki/A7V)

645.

A massive earthquake struck Japan in 1923, causing a fire tornado that incinerated 38,000 people in 15 minutes and was so hot that people's feet were melted to the ground and they could not run away.

Reference: (https://en.wikipedia.org/wiki/1923_Great_Kant%C5%8D_earthquake)

646.

Despite his lady's man reputation, Elvis Presley avoided intercourse with most if not all of his early girlfriends, even Priscilla before they were married. One biographer suggested that The King developed an extreme fear of STDs during his military service.

Reference: (https://en.wikipedia.org/wiki/Personal_relationships_of_Elvis_Presley)

647.

The White House has a Chief Calligrapher, as well as a "Graphics and Calligraphy Office".

Reference: (https://en.wikipedia.org/wiki/White_House_Chief_Calligrapher)

648.

After the U.S. Civil War, the U.S. filed financial claims against Great Britain, claiming that their support for the Confederacy prolonged the war. One Senator demanded a payment of $2 billion, but offered that the U.K. could just turn over Canada as payment instead.

Reference: (https://en.wikipedia.org/wiki/Charles_Sumner#CSS_Alabama_claims)

649.

The Black Cat is an IWW symbol used as a code image for "sabotage"; to slow production on purpose as a means to striking.

Reference: (https://www.iww.org/history/icons/black_cat)

650.

Before fame, Bruce Springsteen acquired his nickname "The Boss" because he took on the task of collecting the band's nightly pay from their club gigs and distributing it amongst his bandmates. Springsteen is not fond of this nickname, due to his dislike of bosses, but has tacitly accepted it.

Reference:(https://en.wikipedia.org/wiki/Bruce_Springsteen#1972%E2%80%931974:_Initial_struggle_for_success)

651.

Edward Dickinson Baker was serving as a U.S. Senator when the U.S. Civil War broke out and re-joined the army as a colonel. He was killed in battle and remains the only sitting U.S. senator ever to be killed in a military engagement.

Reference: (https://en.wikipedia.org/wiki/Edward_Dickinson_Baker)

652.

In 1948, in the U.S., pregnant women were not allowed to be teachers in 57% of the public school districts because, "the sight of pregnant women would unfavorably influence students", and because, "pregnant teachers' minds would not be on their work."

Reference: (https://www.law.georgetown.edu/library/collections/gender-legal-history/glh-summary.cfm?glhID=FF2BA1A8-9057-B8B0-277512F8CB54510F)

653.

Ruth Graham's gravestone says: "End of Construction...Thank you for your Patience."

Reference: (http://kenpierpont.com/2012/11/ruth-grahams-gravestone/)

654.

The term "canola oil" is short for "Canada Oil low acid," a name coined to avoid the less marketable word for the product, "rapeseed oil".

Reference: (https://en.wikipedia.org/wiki/Vegetable_oil#History)

655.

Alan Moore preemptively disowns all filmed adaptations of his work and stated, "I'm never going to watch this fucking thing", when speaking about the film adaptation of "Watchmen."

Reference: (https://www.filmink.com.au/the-making-of-watchmen/)

656.

Students in Tampere, Finland try to drive their rival city Turku in the Baltic by jumping in the market square.

Reference: (https://en.wikipedia.org/wiki/Tampere#City_rivalry_with_Turku)

657.

Guests at the first Academy Awards ceremony ate broiled chicken on toast.

Reference: (https://www.telegraph.co.uk/films/2016/05/16/the-first-oscars-what-happened-in-1929/)

658.

Mr. Robot actor Rami Malek has an identical twin called Sami Malek, who works as a teacher. They occasionally swap places.

Reference: (https://www.youtube.com/watch?v=HvBwJrc_-ns)

659.

For every 2% increase in trans-fat calories consumed daily, the risk of heart disease rises by 23%.

Reference: (https://www.health.harvard.edu/staying-healthy/the-truth-about-fats-bad-and-good)

660.

While serving a prison sentence early in his criminal career, Clyde Barrow, of Bonnie and Clyde, convinced another inmate to help him avoid hard labor by chopping off two of his toes with an axe. Unfortunately, this choice was made in haste and he would be released a mere six days later.

Reference: (https://en.wikipedia.org/wiki/Bonnie_and_Clyde#Clyde_Barrow)

661.

After Endal's owner was knocked out of a wheelchair by a passing car, Endal put him in the recovery position, covered him with a blanket from his wheelchair, retrieved his phone from under the car, and went into a nearby hotel to get help.

Reference: (https://en.wikipedia.org/wiki/Endal)

662.

It took the Dick Milmarth 20 days to win the 1973 Iditarod race. It took last year's winner, Mitch Seavey, only 8 days.

Reference: (http://iditarod.com/about/champions-records/)

663.

The pattern you see when you take a photo of an electronic screen with a digital camera is known as the Moiré pattern.

Reference: (https://en.wikipedia.org/wiki/Moir%C3%A9_pattern)

664.

Francisci Macías Nguema, first President of Equatorial Guinea, once had about 150 of his opponents executed on Christmas Eve by soldiers dressed in Santa Claus outfits at the football stadium in Malabo, while listening to "Those Were the Days" by Mary Hopkin.

Reference: (https://en.wikipedia.org/wiki/Francisco_Mac%C3%ADas_Nguema)

665.

Tiger Woods tried to bribe ex-wife Elin Nordegren with $55 million to stay married for two more years but it didn't work.

Reference: (http://www.thefuss.co.uk/celebrity-prenups/)

666.

While wild puffer fish are poisonous, ones raised in captivity and fed foods that don't contain tetrodotoxin are not poisonous.

Reference: (https://www.practicalfishkeeping.co.uk/features/articles/why-are-pufferfish-poisonous)

667.

Some languages, like Native Australian and Dravidian languages, have two forms of first person plural pronoun "we"; one that includes the addressee and one that doesn't, while English and most European languages, only have a single pronoun for both purposes. This is called Clusivity.

Reference: (https://en.wikipedia.org/wiki/Clusivity)

668.

Bees traveled 7 miles to visit their beekeeper Marget Bells funeral.

Reference: (https://trendingposts.net/trending-weird-news/these-incidents-seems-like-bizarre-but-are-actually-true/)

669.

Monkeys display metacognitive abilities, which means that they are aware of their own thought process and knowledge, and seek to actively control it.

Reference: (https://www.psychologicalscience.org/news/releases/do-monkeys-know-when-they-dont-know-something.html)

670.

The state of Indiana attempted to legally define pi as 3.2 in 1897. It is known as the "Indiana Pi Bill".

Reference: (https://en.wikipedia.org/wiki/Indiana_Pi_Bill)

671.

September 11th is the beginning of a New Year in the Ethiopian calendar.

Reference: (https://www.officeholidays.com/countries/ethiopia/ethiopian-new-year.php)

672.

There are 33 Shakespeare gardens in the world that only cultivate plants which were mentioned in the works of William Shakespeare.

Reference: (https://en.wikipedia.org/wiki/Shakespeare_garden)

673.

One of the first Squad Drills that you learn in the U.S. Army is, "Patrolling TTP for Crossing Linear Danger Areas", or, how to cross the road.

Reference: (https://www.globalsecurity.org/military/library/report/call/call_97-15_ctc3q1a.htm)

674.

In 1897, London, there was a fleet of more than 75 electric taxis.

Reference: (http://www.wired.co.uk/article/1897-electric-car)

675.

Etruscan and Roman concept of Saeculum is the time frame where a human group renews its population completely, from a certain starting point to everyone alive at that point eventually dying. Rome had 24 and Egypt had 30. According to mythos, only a set amount are allotted to different civilizations.

Reference: (https://sashat.me/2017/07/27/in-saecula-saeculorum/)

676.

One of New York's first crime bosses was a Prussian immigrant known as Mother Mandelbaum. She built up a criminal empire worth millions, ran a school to teach kids how to become successful pickpockets and thieves, and functioned as one most prominent hostesses for New York's high society.

Reference: (https://www.smithsonianmag.com/history/the-life-and-crimes-of-old-mother-mandelbaum-71693582/)

677.

The longest time between twins being born is 87 days.

Reference: (https://www.mirror.co.uk/news/real-life-stories/miracle-twins-born-record-87-1857782)

678.

If you put all the roads on Earth in one straight line and pointed it into space, it would almost reach Venus.

Reference: (https://www.reddit.com/user/Brettwurst)

679.

There are over a million ancient Sumerian texts, which is the earliest human writing. Only 30,000 have been translated, with most sitting unread in museum warehouses for centuries.

Reference: (https://en.wikipedia.org/w/index.php?title=Cuneiform_script&oldid=829368191)

680.

In the WNBA, the maximum salary is $107,000 per year for a star player. LeBron James makes more in a year than all players in the WNBA combined.

Reference: (https://en.wikipedia.org/wiki/Professional_sports#Sports_salaries)

681.

There was a real life "Gone Girl." In 1954, Joan Flynn disappeared. She had checked out multiple books on murders and disappearances. One theory is that she staged her own murder for her husband to find and ran away to start a new life. She has never been found.

Reference: (https://morbidology.com/gone-girl-joan-risch/)

682.

In Minnesota, people involved in certain DWI and DUI incidents obtain special registration plates that always begin with the letter "W"; there are called "Whiskey Plates."

Reference: (http://www.dwiguys.com/whiskey-plates/)

683.

Weasels are theorized to hypnotize their prey by doing a strange "war dance".

Reference: (https://www.youtube.com/watch?v=xsGs6oEGxJM)

684.

Chinese toddlers traditionally wore split-crotch pants instead of diapers, so they could go whenever they needed to and didn't need changing.

Reference: (https://www.pbs.org/newshour/health/let-these-globe-trotting-lessons-in-potty-training-flush-your-parental-worries-away)

685.

Finland trains elite soldiers in Lapland in preparation for a future war with neighboring Russia. The two countries share an 833 mile border and were in conflict during World War II.

Reference: (https://www.outsideonline.com/2267491/red-dawn-lapland)

686.

Thomas Edison's last breath is held in a vial in Michigan.

Reference: (https://www.smithsonianmag.com/smart-news/one-thomas-edisons-last-breaths-test-tube-180953819/)

687.

King George III had a mental disorder called porphyria that caused his madness, and also may have turned his urine blue.

Reference:(http://archive.boston.com/yourlife/health/mental/articles/2005/08/01/madness_of_king_george_iii_may_have_been_his_doctors_fault/)

688.

Helicopter blades glow in the sand due to the Kopp Etchells Effect.

Reference: (https://www.theatlantic.com/technology/archive/2011/02/picture-of-the-day-kopp-etchells-effect-on-military-helicopters/70765/)

689.

Dr. Seuss wrote a picture book with seven naked female protagonists that was intended only for adults.

Reference: (https://en.wikipedia.org/wiki/The_Seven_Lady_Godivas)

690.

Tour skating is a long distance form of ice skating on natural ice in which skaters commonly travel 60 to 80 kilometers, and sometimes even over 150 kilometers, in one day.

Reference: (https://en.wikipedia.org/wiki/Tour_skating)

691.

The oldest recorded joke in history is about a fart.

Reference: (https://uk.reuters.com/article/uk-britain-joke-life/worlds-oldest-joke-traced-back-to-1900-bc-idUKL129052420080731)

692.

After being fatally shot in 1996, Tupac Shakur's last and only words to assisting police were "fuck you". He refused to say anything else.

Reference: (https://edition.cnn.com/2014/05/23/showbiz/celebrity-news-gossip/tupac-last-words-rs/index.html)

693.

In the late 1960s, some researchers reported that catnip gave people a marijuana-like high when smoked, but it turned out they had simply mixed up the two plants.

Reference: (https://www.popsci.com/science/article/2013-04/catnip-effects-humans#page-2)

694.

UFC fighters can apply 12 times as much pressure in a choke hold than a snake.

Reference: (https://www.bjjee.com/videos/comparing-the-choking-strength-of-a-python-fedor-emelianenko/)

695.

Former King Bhumibol of Thailand ordered the massacre of Thammasat University students after some of their schoolmates mocked his son, the current King of Thailand.

Reference: (https://en.wikipedia.org/wiki/Thammasat_University_massacre)

696.

Cats have almost twice the amount of neurons as dogs and can be allergic to humans.

Reference: (http://mentalfloss.com/article/55726/20-fun-facts-about-our-mysterious-feline-friends)

697.

There is a Danish church built in 1806 in the Indian state of West Bengal.

Reference: (https://en.wikipedia.org/wiki/St._Olav%27s_Church,_Serampore)

698.

The tuxedo jacket is named after the exclusive Tuxedo Club in upstate New York. "Tuxedo" being an anglicization of an Algonquin word meaning "place of the bear".

Reference: (http://www.townandcountrymag.com/society/tradition/amp833/tuxedo-jacket-history/)

699.

The Jonestown cult, Peoples Temple, had a chimp mascot named Mr. Muggs, who they shot in the head during the mass suicide.

Reference: (https://calisphere.org/item/ark:/13030/kt3p3036w1/)

700.

The Wyoming Department of Transportation uses military-grade artillery to control avalanches.

Reference: (http://billingsgazette.com/news/state-and-regional/wyoming/wydot-leasing-howitzer-for-avalanche-gun-teton-pass-to-close/article_779b96b4-5ada-5804-9bfe-4b1130d7a0fb.html)

701.

Richard Lawrence was a man who failed his mission to assassinate President Andrew Jackson because both of his pistols misfired. Jackson then beat Lawrence with his cane and Lawrence was detained.

Reference:(https://en.wikipedia.org/wiki/Richard_Lawrence_(failed_assassin)#Assassination_attempt)

702.

David Cross, Tobias from "Arrested Development," fought to keep his characters now signature mustache in the show.

Reference: (https://www.youtube.com/watch?v=y5Wr_BpeBKc)

703.

In the 800s, the Emperor of Japan outlawed meat consumption and capital punishment.

Reference: (https://en.wikipedia.org/wiki/Emperor_Saga#Legacy)

704.

While searching for 3 missing activists in the "Mississippi Burning" murders the FBI searched area swamps. Instead of those men's bodies, Navy divers who dragged the river discovered the bodies of a 14-year old boy, 2 other black activists, and 5 other black men who remained unidentified.

Reference: (http://www.crmvet.org/tim/tim64b.htm#1964csg)

705.

The Loco-Motion is one of nine songs to reach number 1 by two different artists.

Reference: (https://en.wikipedia.org/wiki/The_Loco-Motion)

706.

Henry Ford and Adolf Hitler were good friends.

Reference:(https://en.wikipedia.org/wiki/Henry_Ford#The_Dearborn_Independent_and_antisemitism)

707.

Japanese-born Koreans were tricked into living in North Korea.

Reference: (https://www.nknews.org/2016/11/how-the-zainichi-koreans-adjusted-to-life-in-north-korea/?c=1519968148807)

708.

The world record for hyperinflation is held by post-World War II Hungary, where prices doubled every 15 hours.

Reference: (https://www.scribd.com/document/267706713/Hanke-Krus-Hyperinflation-Table-May-2013)

709.

Silicon Valley is not ranked first in the country in terms of concentration of IT employment, it's actually the Baltimore-Washington region.

Reference: (https://en.wikipedia.org/wiki/Business_in_Maryland#Workforce)

710.

The buildings within the Los Angeles cityscape of Blade Runner 2049 were not CGI, but miniatures.

Reference: (https://www.youtube.com/watch?v=sLxxbfsj8IM)

711.

Russia made a movie adaption of “The Hobbit” in 1985 called "The Fabulous Journey of Mr. Bilbo Baggins, The Hobbit, Across the Wild Land, Through the Dark Forest, Beyond the Misty Mountains. There and Back Again".

Reference: (https://en.wikipedia.org/wiki/The_Hobbit_(1985_film))

712.

In 1986, defunct electronics store Silo offered a stereo system for "299 bananas." Customers took it literally, Silo was forced to honor the ad and lost over $10,000.

Reference: (http://wikipedia.org/wiki/Silo_(store))

713.

Ron Jeremy in an extra in the original “Ghost Busters.”

Reference: (http://www.indiewire.com/2012/06/5-things-you-might-not-know-about-ghostbusters-109754/)

714.

Before he was radicalized, Osama Bin Laden loved westerns and was an aspiring cowboy. He could also be seen strutting around Abbottabad, Pakistan in the years before his death in a cowboy hat.

Reference: (https://www.marketwatch.com/story/why-osama-bin-laden-wore-a-cowboy-hat-2013-07-10)

715.

An island was christened a war ship by the British Navy during a French blockade. The HMS Diamond Rock was fortified with cannons and spent 17 months hammering any passing French ships, and to this day anyone in the British Navy is required to salute the rock when they pass it.

Reference: (http://military.wikia.com/wiki/Diamond_Rock)

716.

It may have started in Sweden, but IKEA is a Dutch-owned company with its headquarters in the Netherlands.

Reference: (https://en.wikipedia.org/wiki/IKEA#Corporate_structure)

717.

In 1941, the U.S Army purchased 17,232 acres in St. Charles County near Weldon Spring, Missouri as part of the World War II defense effort. Still standing today there are just over 100 bunkers that were built to store high explosives.

Reference: (http://www.romeofthewest.com/2009/09/weldon-spring-site.html?m=1)

718.

House Speaker, Dennis Hastert welcomed China to the World Trade Organization by cracking open a ceremonial fortune cookie.

Reference: (https://www.bizjournals.com/sanfrancisco/stories/2000/06/05/editorial2.html)

719.

Stevie Wonder's first name is actually Stevland.

Reference: (https://www.cnn.com/2013/06/07/us/stevie-wonder-fast-facts/index.html)

720.

The oldest known grave for a "pet cat" is on Cyprus, dating from 9,500 years ago.

Reference: (http://news.bbc.co.uk/1/hi/sci/tech/3611453.stm)

721.

Vice President Johnson had a fake thermostat control in his state room on Air Force Two that was installed in an effort to stop him coming into the cockpit and messing with the temperature controls.

Reference: (http://www.museumofflight.org/aircraft/boeing-vc-137b-707-120sam-970-air-force-one)

722.

Yoko Ono was a famous performance artist in her own right.

Reference: (https://www.moma.org/learn/moma_learning/yoko-ono-cut-piece-1964)

723.

Hanna Barbera adapted "The Last of the Mohicans" into an animated film in 1975.

Reference: (https://www.youtube.com/watch?v=zW8aC0fnCuQ)

724.

Jeffrey Dahmer's parents, noticing their son's abnormalities at a young age, let him name his younger brother, David, in an attempt to have Jeffrey feel more involved.

Reference: (https://www.youtube.com/watch?v=Xe5OixqeLVw&t=3m40s)

725.

In his 1985 novel "Robots and Empire", Isaac Asimov added a Zeroth Law of Robotics which posited that, "A robot may not harm humanity, or, by inaction, allow humanity to come to harm."

Reference: (https://en.wikipedia.org/wiki/Three_Laws_of_Robotics#Zeroth_Law_added)

726.

There is a method to create a rhombus and square using magnetic balls and sticks.

Reference: (https://www.youtube.com/watch?v=4rj-T5AKwOw&feature=youtu.be)

727.

Christian BDSM is a real thing.

Reference: (http://www.christiandomesticdiscipline.com/home.html)

728.

The U.S. state of Hawaii holds both records for the state with both the highest low and the state with the lowest high temperature ever recorded. Hawaii has never seen a temperature above 98°F when even Alaska has hit 100°F.

Reference: (https://wikivisually.com/wiki/U.S._state_temperature_extremes)

729.

The phrase, "the die is cast", is from a Julius Caesar quote referring to gaming dice. It is not from the die casting manufacturing process as previously thought.

Reference: (https://en.wikipedia.org/wiki/Alea_iacta_est)

730.

When Halle Berry won a Worst Actor Razzie award for her role in "Catwoman," she showed up in person to collect the award. She spoke while holding her Academy Award from "Monster's Ball" in one hand and the Razzie in the other.

Reference: (https://en.wikipedia.org/wiki/Halle_Berry#Recent_work)

731.

Six years before the actual game, the television show Quantum Leap predicted that the Pittsburgh Steelers would be down by three points in Super Bowl XXX. The Steelers were down 20-17 in the fourth quarter.

Reference: (https://youtu.be/HFLaGozCjUE#t=64s)

732.

Ursula the Sea Witch is inspired, in both appearance and demeanor, by drag legend and John Waters muse Divine.

Reference: (https://news.avclub.com/read-this-how-divine-inspired-ursula-the-sea-witch-1798243255)

733.

Some appliances keep time by relying on AC frequency. Due to a disruption it made some clocks lose time.

Reference: (http://www.bbc.co.uk/news/world-europe-43321113)

734.

In June 1940, France proposed merging the countries of France and England into the Franco-British union, with a stated goal of defeating Nazi Germany.

Reference: (https://en.wikipedia.org/wiki/Franco-British_Union)

735.

Two men robbed and murdered two other men in March, 1883, in Lexington, California, which is now a ghost town.

Reference: (https://en.wikipedia.org/wiki/Lexington_murders)

736.

A young Steve Martin was captured on a home video at Disneyland in 1956. He had a job handing out flyers to guests.

Reference: (https://www.youtube.com/watch?v=jZKHnAT_0c0)

737.

The FDA allow five rodent hairs in every 18 ounce jar of peanut butter, while frozen berries can contain up to four larvae or 10 whole insects per 500 grams.

Reference: (http://www.bbc.co.uk/programmes/articles/fQz5fzDFvsSVzNDBRptv5P/seven-weird-things-you-re-eating-without-realising-and-why)

738.

Victoria's Secret comes from "Victoria" after Queen Victoria, to associate with the refinement of the era, and "Secret", which was what was hidden underneath the clothes.

Reference: (https://www.wikipedia.org/wiki/Victoria%27s_Secret)

739.

Hairy Black Holes is the hypothesis that Black Holes have “soft hairs” to preserve information falling in.

Reference: (http://www.techtimes.com/articles/128955/20160130/the-hairy-black-hole-hypothesis-black-holes-have-soft-hairs-to-preserve-information-falling-in.htm)

740.

Sir Frederic Leighton is the first painter who was made a Baron in the U.K. This became the shortest peerage in history as he died 1 day later without an heir.

Reference: (https://en.wikipedia.org/wiki/Frederic_Leighton#Biography)

741.

Car crash themed songs emerged as a popular pop and rock music teenage tragedy theme during the 1950s and 1960s, at a time when the number of people being killed in vehicle collisions was rising fast in many countries.

Reference: (https://en.wikipedia.org/wiki/List_of_car_crash_songs)

742.

Some humans on Earth irrationally believe their genitals are shrinking. The disorder is called "koro".

Reference: (https://io9.gizmodo.com/5944722/koro-syndrome-the-irrational-fear-of-lethal-genital-shrinkage)

743.

Edmund Hillary was the first person to reach both the South and North Poles and summit Everest.

Reference: (https://en.wikipedia.org/wiki/Edmund_Hillary#After_Everest)

744.

In the 18th century, many prominent voices were concerned by an “epidemic” affecting young people whereby they were spending too much time reading books. It was diagnosed as a dangerous disease called, “reading rage, reading fever, reading mania or reading lust.”

Reference: (https://www.historytoday.com/frank-furedi/media%E2%80%99s-first-moral-panic)

745.

Scottish crofters are likely to disappear in the coming years as few want to live in isolation and work the land in harsh and demanding conditions of the far north-west of Scotland.

Reference: (https://www.independent.co.uk/arts-entertainment/folk-who-live-on-the-edge-the-highland-crofter-is-traditionally-a-long-suffering-victim-of-1436227.html)

746.

According to secret documents issued to interrogators at Guantanamo Bay, "possession of the F-91W suggests the wearer has been trained in bomb making by al-Qaeda in Afghanistan", after United States Military intelligence officials identified the watch being used when constructing time bombs.

Reference: (https://en.wikipedia.org/wiki/Casio_F-91W)

747.

In 2015, Costco sold more than 128 million hot dogs in their food courts. That's four times the amount of hot dogs sold in all MLB ballparks combined.

Reference: (http://www.mashed.com/103084/dont-know-costcos-1-hot-dog/)

748.

In 1953, the Cincinnati Reds changed their name to the Redlegs in response to anti-communist sentiment in America.

Reference: (https://en.wikipedia.org/wiki/1953_Cincinnati_Redlegs_season)

749.

Malaysia proposed that the UN Security Council set up an international tribunal to prosecute those deemed responsible for the downing of a Malaysia Airlines Flight. 298 people died over Ukraine when hit by a Russian Anti-Aircraft Rocket in 2014; the resolution was vetoed by Russia.

Reference: (https://en.wikipedia.org/wiki/Malaysia_Airlines_Flight_17)

750.

When a Tanomani tribe member dies, they burn the body and mix the ash powder into plantain soup, to be eaten by the guests.

Reference: (https://garfors.com/2016/12/25-strange-customs-and-traditions-html/)

751.

In 2009, due to low funds, workers at the zoo in Gaza City painted black stripes onto donkeys to convince schoolchildren they were zebras. None of the children caught on.

Reference: (http://latimesblogs.latimes.com/unleashed/2009/10/gaza-donkeys-zebras.html)

752.

Siwash the Marine duck was the mascot of the First Battalion of the Tenth Marine Regiment and later the entire Second Marine Division during World War II. He went ashore with the Marines at the Battle of Tarawa in 1943. There, he was cited by fellow Marines for fighting a Japanese-owned rooster.

Reference: (http://www.leatherneck.com/forums/archive/index.php/t-47643.html)

753.

Rumble strutting is a guinea pig behavior in which they strut around each other shaking their butts low to emit a rumbling sound. It can sound a lot like purring, but it's part of their herd rituals to determine dominance.

Reference: (https://en.wikipedia.org/wiki/Guinea_pig)

754.

C.S. Lewis, John F. Kennedy and Aldous Huxley all died on the exact same day, November 22nd, 1963.

Reference: (https://en.wikipedia.org/wiki/C._S._Lewis)

755.

Liechtenstein has won the most Olympic medals per capita of any country, with nearly one medal for every 3,600 inhabitants.

Reference: (https://en.wikipedia.org/wiki/Liechtenstein_at_the_Olympics)

756.

Alanis Morissettes' Jagged Little Pill has sold more copies that Sgt. Peppers Lonely Hearts Club Band.

Reference: (https://en.wikipedia.org/wiki/List_of_best-selling_albums#30%E2%80%9339_million_copies)

757.

35% of millennials own their own house in the U.S.

Reference: (http://www.bbc.com/news/world-39512599)

758.

We can identify a friend's voice after hearing just two words.

Reference: (https://www.huffingtonpost.com/entry/voice-recognition-study_us_5617c7b2e4b0082030a2071d)

759.

Qırmızı Qəsəbə is a city in Azerbaijan where Jews make up a larger share of the population than any other city in the world, including Israel and America. It is considered to be the last surviving Jewish shtetl, pre-modern insular Jewish community, in the world.

Reference:(https://en.wikipedia.org/wiki/Q%C4%B1rm%C4%B1z%C4%B1_Q%C9%99s%C9%99b%C9%99)

760.

Sir Arthur Conan Doyle, writer of Sherlock Holmes, ingested a small amount of a poison and kept increasing the amount every day until he could no longer stand the ill effects. He stopped his experiment after being stricken by persistent diarrhea, severe frontal headache, and great depression.

Reference: (https://en.wikipedia.org/wiki/Gelsemium#Self-experimentation)

761.

While working on "Snowpiercer," director Bong Joon-ho found the hardest part about working with Chris Evans was finding different ways to hide, "all that muscle mass."

Reference: (https://en.wikipedia.org/wiki/Snowpiercer#Cast)

762.

A bunch of hackers compromised an epileptic support forum and placed seizure inducing gifs on the site for the fun of it.

Reference: (https://www.cbsnews.com/news/epilepsy-site-hacked-with-seizure-images/)

763.

The FBI kept 2,403 pages of records on Frank Sinatra for his Mafia ties.

Reference: (https://en.wikipedia.org/wiki/Personal_life_of_Frank_Sinatra)

764.

The do-not-call list does not work anymore; which has allowed massive robocalls to happen.

Reference: (https://www.technologyreview.com/s/602284/the-do-not-call-list-has-a-gaping-hole)

765.

Clara Blandick was only eight years older than Billie Burke. Ideally, Blandick would've played Em and Glinda, but the studio wanted someone who looked younger to play the good witch in "Wizard of Oz."

Reference: (https://en.wikipedia.org/wiki/Clara_Blandick)

766.

Adrian Carton de Wiart got shot on multiple occasions and tore off two of his fingers when a doctor refused to amputate them. He also survived two plane crashes and tunneled out of a prisoner of war camp, among other stunning achievements.

Reference: (http://www.bbc.com/news/magazine-30685433)

767.

A 2008 study of the British authorities' Convict Transportation Registers from 1788 to 1868 estimated that 22 percent of living Australians had a convict ancestor.

Reference: (http://www.abc.net.au/news/2007-07-25/online-records-highlight-australias-convict-past/2512534)

768.

The position of the exit number relative to the exit sign indicates which side of the highway the exit is on.

Reference: (https://lifehacker.com/5953223/quickly-tell-whether-the-highway-exit-will-be-on-the-left-or-the-right)

769.

Contrary to popular belief, photosensitive epilepsy, the form of epilepsy where seizures are triggered by flashing lights, is actually rare; it only accounts for about 3% of all cases.

Reference: (https://en.wikipedia.org/wiki/Causes_of_seizures#Lights)

770.

Sloths are really slow for survival reasons. It has to do with their slow digestion process.

Reference: (https://www.interestinganswers.com/animals/why-are-sloths-so-slow/)

771.

Scientists aren't just working on lab-grown meat, but lab-grown milk as well, which will yield vegan-friendly cheese, butter, and ice cream, and also reduce the carbon footprint of the dairy industry.

Reference: (https://www.theguardian.com/environment/2016/sep/13/animal-free-dairy-products-move-a-step-closer-to-market)

772.

There are particles called "Spooky Particles", which are also known as Quantum Entangled Photons.

Reference: (https://helios.gsfc.nasa.gov/qa_gp_tp.html#spooky)

773.

Before killing Cecil the lion, Walter Palmer was penalized $2,938 for illegally killing a black bear in Wisconsin in 2006 and he tried to bribe his guides $20,000 to cover it up.

Reference: (http://abcnews.go.com/US/photos-black-bear-illegally-hunted-dentist-walter-palmer/story?id=33067963)

774.

The first chancellor of the federal republic of Germany, Konrad Adenauer, invented a kind of soy sausage during World War I because the Germans had a lack of pork supply.

Reference: (https://www.theguardian.com/world/the-h-word/2014/jul/07/saving-the-bacon-during-the-first-world-war)

775.

Garuda Indonesia Flight 421 was a mostly successful river landing of a passenger aircraft that took place a full seven years before the accident that came to be known as the "Miracle on the Hudson".

Reference: (https://en.wikipedia.org/wiki/Garuda_Indonesia_Flight_421)

776.

The Y chromosome in humans has lost nearly 97% of its original genetic composition over the last 300 million years, degenerating at a rate of 4.6 genes per million years.

Reference: (https://www.ncbi.nlm.nih.gov/pmc/articles/PMC1692900/)

777.

J. Peterman's clothing company that Elaine Benes worked for on Seinfeld is a real company. Their clothes really do come with whimsical stories.

Reference: (https://www.jpeterman.com/)

778.

There is "missile-proof" Russian tank that can block projectiles moving at hypersonic speeds with kinetic energy charge interceptors. It uses an advanced "millimeter-wave" radar system to protect itself from all sides.

Reference: (https://en.wikipedia.org/wiki/T-14_Armata)

779.

Canada's criminal code states that any person who challenges, provokes, or accepts a challenge to fight a duel is guilty of an indictable offense and can be imprisoned up to two years.

Reference: (http://laws-lois.justice.gc.ca/eng/acts/C-46/page-10.html#h-19)

780.

In a 2012 survey, 30% of women said they experienced pain the last time they had vaginal sex. A large proportion did not tell their partner when they were in pain.

Reference: (https://www.ncbi.nlm.nih.gov/pubmed/25648245)

781.

France's former African colonies are still required to keep their financial reserves in a French bank earning 0.75% interest. Some call this a continuing colonial tax on the former colonies.

Reference: (https://www.bloomberg.com/news/articles/2014-04-17/african-monetary-union-stirs-criticism-of-france)

782.

Alexander the Great's army conquered the world while wearing armor made of linen that could stop any arrow made at the time.

Reference: (https://www.newyorker.com/books/joshua-rothman/how-to-make-your-own-greek-armor)

783.

Humans were around for 194,000 years before civilization as we know it began.

Reference: (https://www.universetoday.com/38125/how-long-have-humans-been-on-earth/)

784.

The iconic actor George C. Scott, who is most famous for his role as General George S. Patton in the film "Patton", is buried in an unmarked grave located to the right of that of fellow actor Walter Matthau.

Reference: (https://en.wikipedia.org/wiki/George_C._Scott)

785.

John Wayne actually went bald in the 1940's and wore a hair piece throughout his career.

Reference: (https://www.youtube.com/watch?v=6w9ewXKG0KY)

786.

The Shadow Realm in “Yu-Gi-Oh!” was made up by 4kids in the English dub of the show for anyone that had died or was seriously injured in the original Japanese anime.

Reference: (http://evil.wikia.com/wiki/Shadow_Realm_(Yu-Gi-Oh!))

787.

In 1971, a 22 year old Gerald Mayo, held at Western Penitentiary in Pittsburgh, tried to take "Satan and His Staff" to a federal court for allegedly, “causing the plaintiff's downfall.”

Reference: (https://loweringthebar.net/case-law-hall-of-fame/mayo)

788.

There are 13 sequels to “The Wonderful Wizard of Oz” by L. Frank Baum.

Reference: (https://en.wikipedia.org/wiki/List_of_Oz_books)

789.

In the 1948 Winter Olympics, a team made up entirely of Canadian Air Force personnel won the gold medal in hockey.

Reference: (https://en.wikipedia.org/wiki/Ottawa_RCAF_Flyers)

790.

The sound you hear when you close a car door is artificially produced using dampeners, following regulation changes 15 years ago.

Reference: (http://news.bbc.co.uk/2/hi/programmes/click_online/9533769.stm)

791.

There is a “Secret Museum” of erotic Pompeian artwork. Since these objects were considered pornographic in the nineteenth century, they were never fully and permanently revealed to the public until 2000.

Reference: (https://en.wikipedia.org/wiki/Secret_Museum,_Naples)

792.

The "He-Gassen" is a series of Japanese scrolls from 1840 containing paintings of fart battles. Some think it was intended to ridicule Europeans but that remains unproven.

Reference: (https://io9.gizmodo.com/5886529/japanese-fart-scrolls-prove-that-human-art-peaked-centuries-ago)

793.

Dancing is banned in Germany on the Christian holy day of Good Friday.

Reference: (https://www.irishtimes.com/news/world/europe/germans-split-over-their-own-good-friday-ban-on-dancing-1.3047998)

794.

Massive World War II era recoilless rifles are used for avalanche control.

Reference: (http://www.nytimes.com/2009/03/20/us/20alta.html)

795.

A group of rabbits is called a "fluffle".

Reference: (https://rabbit.org/basic-rabbit-facts/)

796.

Apple seeds do not produce the same apples as their parent. To keep the same flavor, apple trees must be grafted. Every Honeycrisp apple you have ever eaten has come from the same tree, just split apart.

Reference: (https://www.starkbros.com/growing-guide/article/science-of-grafting)

797.

Tom Green won 5 Rasberry Awards for "Freddie Got Fingered" in 2002. He showed up in a white Cadillac, rolled out his own red carpet, and had to be dragged off stage because he wouldn't stop playing the harmonica.

Reference: (https://www.youtube.com/watch?v=8v92IS-Aghw&t=6s)

798.

14 states have an official seashell; the state dog of Wisconsin is the American Water Spaniel; only 3 states, Texas, Oklahoma and Virginia, have official state bats; and Oregon is the lone state with an official state microbe.

Reference: (https://en.wikipedia.org/wiki/Lists_of_United_States_state_symbols)

799.

Clark Kent, Superman's alter ego, was likely modeled after science fiction writer, Walter Dennis. Dennis was asked by Joe Shuster if it would be alright to use his likeness for Kent.

Reference: (http://www.noblemania.com/2014/03/clark-kents-grandson.html?m=1)

800.

While scanning Neil Armstrong and Buzz Aldrin's ship, the Columbia, museum staff found the astronauts had scribbled graffiti on the walls and around the mission controls which included calculations, calendars, and other notes throughout the duration of the trip.

Reference: (https://airandspace.si.edu/newsroom/press-releases/smithsonian-3-d-project-sheds-new-light-astronaut-graffiti-found-museum%E2%80%99s?id=400)

801.

The richest family in the U.K. is Indian.

Reference: (https://en.wikipedia.org/wiki/List_of_British_billionaires_by_net_worth)

802.

Before becoming a police officer, Christopher Dorner returned a purse with $8,000 to a Korean church saying, "It's an integrity thing".

Reference: (http://www.enidnews.com/news/local_news/ene-archives-vance-students-turn-in-lost-church-money/article_6f6f6cfe-3558-5e8a-a828-d4deec5c0a17.html#cb=fdd0205ed56568&origin=http%3A%2F%2Fenidnews.com%2Ff34619491750dc8&domain=enidnews.com&relation=parent&error=not_authorized)

803.

There's a company called Ethisphere that designates the "World's Most Ethical Companies". Awards are given after completing a short questionnaire and paying $11,000.

Reference: (https://www.worldsmostethicalcompanies.com/)

804.

There is such a thing as International Men's Day. November 19th was chosen to celebrate how on that date, in 1989, Trinidad and Tobago's soccer team had united the country with their endeavors to qualify for the soccer World Cup.

Reference: (https://en.wikipedia.org/wiki/International_Men%27s_Day)

805.

Chimp Frodo beat up Jane Goodall, fathered a baby with his own mother and also ate a human baby.

Reference: (http://blog.michael-lawrence-wilson.com/2014/01/19/frodo-30-june-1976-10-november-2013/)

806.

Kurt Busch is the last full time NASCAR Cup driver to have raced Dale Earnhardt.

Reference: (https://en.wikipedia.org/wiki/2001_Daytona_500)

807.

Seasonal Affective Dissorder, also known as seasonal depression or winter blues, is abbreviated as SAD, sometimes even Winter SAD.

Reference: (https://en.wikipedia.org/wiki/Seasonal_affective_disorder)

808.

The exact center of the northwest hemisphere of the Earth is marked in the middle of a farm field in the tiny town of Poniatowski, Wisconsin. Two of the other three central locations are in oceans. The other is in a mountainous region of China.

Reference: (https://www.atlasobscura.com/places/45-x-90-geographical-marker)

809.

Dylan McDermott was 5 years old when his mom died of a gunshot in 1967. Her death was ruled an accident at the time but Dylan was able to get the cold case reopened 40 years later. Through the new investigation, they discovered a cover-up and that her boyfriend, a known gangster, had murdered her.

Reference: (https://www.today.com/news/police-actor-dylan-mcdermotts-mother-was-murdered-1967-844276)

810.

In 1859, the largest solar storm on record, the Carrington Event, would devastate modern technology, and caused the northern lights to be seen as far south as Cuba.

Reference: (https://news.nationalgeographic.com/news/2011/03/110302-solar-flares-sun-storms-earth-danger-carrington-event-science/)

811.

"Sesame Street" introduced a Muppet with a dad in jail.

Reference: (http://www.nydailynews.com/entertainment/tv-movies/sesame-street-introduces-muppet-dad-jail-article-1.1376845)

812.

After Nelson Mandela's death, NHL goalie Jonathan Bernier gave a TV interview in which he referred to Mandela as, "one of the most-known athletes" and "a great guy off and on the ice".

Reference: (https://globalnews.ca/news/1715103/bernier-embarrassed-after-saying-nelson-mandela-was-athlete/)

813.

Dolphins and bats both hunt their prey by emitting high-pitched sounds and listening for the echoes. This ability arose independently in each group of mammals from the same genetic mutations.

Reference: (http://www.sciencemag.org/news/2013/09/bats-and-dolphins-evolved-echolocation-same-way)

814.

The island Nikumaroro, where Amelia Earhart is thought to have lived out her last few weeks in 1937, was colonized from 1938 to 1963.

Reference: (https://en.wikipedia.org/wiki/Nikumaroro#Amelia_Earhart)

815.

Fucking Hell is a German Pilsner or pale lager with an alcohol content of 4.9%. It is named after the village of Fucking in Austria; hell is the German word for "pale" and a typical description of this kind of beer.

Reference: (https://en.wikipedia.org/wiki/Fucking,_Austria)

816.

"Baby Got Back" by Sir Mix-a-lot was a call to see beauty in diversity. Sir Mix-a-lot used the song to blame the media for skewing the notion of beauty and hoped his music would empower women of all shapes and sizes.

Reference: (https://www.npr.org/2017/05/08/527448477/sir-mix-a-lot-on-25-years-of-baby-got-back)

817.

For Spiderman: Homecoming they specifically animated the CGI to look like it was Tom Holland in the suit. It worked so well that Tom himself thought the completely CGI test was him moving around.

Reference: (https://www.youtube.com/watch?v=AWUvNY3Gu-0&feature=youtu.be&t=1m26s)

818.

On March 10th, 1982, the "Krononauts" awaited the arrival of "visitors from the futures" as the planets moved into alignment.

Reference: (http://www.nytimes.com/1982/03/11/us/the-night-the-planets-were-aligned-with-baltimore-lunacy.html)

819.

Rain Scent occurs from geosmin and oil.

Reference: (https://en.wikipedia.org/wiki/Petrichor)

820.

Water's melting point is 0.00251 9°C and the boiling point is 99.9743°C. The temperature scale with the melting point as 0 and the boiling point as 100 is the centigrade temperature scale.

Reference: (http://www.idc-online.com/technical_references/pdfs/chemical_engineering/Water_properties.pdf)

821.

The word "awful" originally meant "inspiring wonder or fear". Now the word has a negative meaning, usually to express disgust.

Reference: (https://en.wikipedia.org/wiki/Semantic_change)

822.

Jerry Lewis directed and starred in "The Day The Clown Cried", a movie about Helmut Doork, a German clown in a Nazi concentration camp who was used to entertain and eventually lead the kids to the gas chambers.

Reference: (https://en.wikipedia.org/wiki/The_Day_the_Clown_Cried)

823.

Joan Murray survived a 14,500 foot fall when her main parachute failed while skydiving. She landed in a fire ant mound. Numerous venomous stings caused an adrenaline rush to keep her heart beating long enough for doctors to assist.

Reference: (http://www.skydiving.com/news/2017/skydiving/female-skydiving-enthusiast-survives-plummeting-14500-feet-onto-fire-ant-mound/)

824.

The first arrest for drunk driving was in 1897 when George Smith slammed his taxi into the side of a building in London. Then, 34 years later in 1932 the first form of the breathalyzer was made where you blew into a balloon filled with chemicals.

Reference: (https://www.history.com/this-day-in-history/londoner-george-smith-gets-caught-driving-drunk)

825.

One episode of the TV series "House" was entirely filmed using Canon EOS 5D DSLR cameras.

Reference: (https://en.wikipedia.org/wiki/Help_Me_(House)#Filming)

826.

International Women's Day was first celebrated in the Soviet Union and used to be called International Working Women's Day until 1975.

Reference: (https://en.wikipedia.org/wiki/International_Women's_Day)

827.

Stoffel is a honey badger in a South African wildlife center who's escaped his enclosure twice to fight the lions in the exhibit beside his, built towers out of rocks and sticks to climb over his wall, and, when introduced with a mate, stood on her head to unlock the gate and get out once again.

Reference: (https://www.youtube.com/watch?v=45EbX3XPuqM&feature=youtu.be&t=1561)

828.

At the University of California, Berkeley, on the first Tuesday of each month from 12 to 1PM during the fall and spring semesters, there is a "Pet Hugs" therapy dog event to provide stress relief to students.

Reference: (https://en.wikipedia.org/wiki/Sproul_Plaza)

829.

Despite producing about 38 billion ballpoint pens each year, China had yet to acquire the technology to produce their own pen tips domestically until 2017.

Reference: (http://www.chinadaily.com.cn/china/2017-01/18/content_27985815.htm)

830.

The first U.S. President to live in the White House was John Adams, the second President of the United States. Adams and his family moved to the White House in 1800.

Reference: (http://www.enchantedlearning.com/history/us/monuments/whitehouse/)

831.

The amount of time it would take Mount Rushmore to erode into unrecognizability, assuming that it is not maintained, is approximately 7.2 million years.

Reference: (https://en.wikipedia.org/wiki/Timeline_of_the_far_future#Human_constructs)

832.

A healthy cat's normal body temperature is between 100°F, or 37.7°C, and 102.5°F, or 39.1°C.

Reference: (https://www.cat-world.com.au/cat-temperature.html)

833.

The first woman to appear in a Shakespeare play did so in 1660, 44 years after Shakespeare's death. Female characters, such as Cleopatra and Juliet, were played by little boys.

Reference: (http://theatreunbound.com/?p=466)

834.

Quipus is the Andean writing system which didn't use ink or paper. Information was encoded in an intricate system of strings of colored yarn tied in a variety of knots. This system survived until just after the Conquistadors.

Reference: (https://www.ancient.eu/Quipu/)

835.

The genetic mutation responsible for alcohol flush reaction may have given an evolutionary edge to the first farming populations that appeared in China 10,000 years ago by making them less susceptible to alcoholism from rice wine.

Reference: (http://healthland.time.com/2010/01/20/red-faced-from-drinking/)

836.

Being tongue-tied is an actual medical condition affecting the tongue, and it can be treated by surgically cutting the "tie".

Reference: (https://www.nhs.uk/conditions/tongue-tie/)

837.

The Mississippi River would today bypass New Orleans on a very different path if not for a complicated, fragile structure built by the Corps of Engineers in the 1950s.

Reference: (https://www.wunderground.com/blog/JeffMasters/americas-achilles-heel-the-mississippi-rivers-old-river-control-st.html)

838.

Anthony Field, from The Wiggles, doesn't wear shoes when he performs because it has helped him battle issues with his health and depression.

Reference: (http://www.foxnews.com/health/2012/02/17/blue-wiggle-describes-road-to-recovery-in-new-memoir.html)

839.

“The New Shadow” is a supposed sequel to Lord of the Rings that told of the reign of Aragorn’s descendant, men turning back to evil, and a plot to oust the king of Gondor. Tolkien quickly abandoned it after writing only 13 pages.

Reference: (http://tolkiengateway.net/wiki/The_New_Shadow)

840.

Green Bay Packers wide receiver Max McGee didn't expect to play in the first Super Bowl in 1967. He showed up hungover and without his helmet. He ended up making a one-handed catch to score the game's first touchdown.

Reference: (https://en.wikipedia.org/wiki/Max_McGee)

841.

The Cardinal Jaime Sin from the Philippines was generally known as, "The greatest sin of all: Cardinal Sin". He was also known to jokingly welcome guests of his home saying: "Welcome to the house of Sin".

Reference: (https://en.wikipedia.org/wiki/Jaime_Sin#References)

842.

The word “Jehovah” is a Latinized derivative of God's given name “YHWH”, this translated abbreviation stemming from 4 Hebrew consonants called the “tetragrammaton” considered too sacred to utter and whose letters were replaced by Latin-speaking Christian scholars.

Reference: (https://www.britannica.com/topic/Yahweh)

843.

At the end of the 17th century, in an attempt to modernize society, Russian Emperor Peter the Great taxed any men who didn't shave their beard. Those that paid the tax carried around a copper or bronze token as proof they had paid.

Reference: (https://www.smithsonianmag.com/smart-news/why-tsar-peter-great-established-beard-tax-180964693/)

844.

Dubai is planning to build a shape shifting skyscraper.

Reference: (http://whatson.ae/dubai/2017/11/rotating-skyscraper-dubai-2020/)

845.

The most successful Bond movie ever is “Thunderball”, released back in 1965. The movie made over $141 million, which amounts to more than $1 billion today when inflation is adjusted.

Reference: (https://www.investopedia.com/slide-show/top-5-bond-movies-inflation/)

846.

The Seventh Day Adventists are the longest living human group in America and one of the longest in the world.

Reference: (https://en.wikipedia.org/wiki/Blue_Zone)

847.

Sherry has nothing to do with cherries, and in fact is made of wine grapes from Andalusia, as any other wine, and fortified with grape spirit. The name is an Anglicization of the name of the town Jerez, where it is originally produced.

Reference: (https://www.sherrynotes.com/sherry-types/)

848.

"Donaldism" is the name for Disney fandom particularly focused on comics and cartoons. The Germans call their society: "D.O.N.A.L.D.", "Deutsche Organisation nichtkommerzieller Anhänger des lauteren Donaldismus", or the German Organization of Non-commercial Devotees of Pure Donaldism.

Reference: (https://www.donald.org/)

849.

In 1941, Rudolph Hess, Deputy Führer of the Nazi party, flew a plane solo from Germany to Scotland behind Hitler's back to try to negotiate peace with Britain, he ran out of fuel parachuted out and landed in a farm, hearing the plane crash the farmer found him and invited him in for a cup of tea.

Reference: (http://www.historyinanhour.com/2011/05/10/rudolph-hess-summary/)

850.

In Switzerland, the percentage of homicide victims by gender is exactly 50% men and 50% women.

Reference: (https://en.wikipedia.org/wiki/Homicide_statistics_by_gender)

851.

Faxlore is how bored office workers passed jokes and memes around via fax before the internet.

Reference: (https://en.wikipedia.org/wiki/Faxlore)

852.

Size differs between the sexes in 49 different animal classes. In 86 percent of these classes, females were the larger sex. Only in mammals and birds is far more common for males to be larger than females.

Reference: (https://www.huffingtonpost.com/daphne-fairbairn/animal-female-size_b_3177995.html)

853.

Thomas Edison filmed one of the first cat videos in 1894 making them fight in a little boxing ring.

Reference: (https://www.smithsonianmag.com/videos/category/history/thomas-edisons-boxing-cats/?no-ist)

854.

Once upon a time, popcorn was explicitly banned from movie theaters.

Reference: (https://www.smithsonianmag.com/arts-culture/why-do-we-eat-popcorn-at-the-movies-475063/)

855.

Three of the top five most valuable companies in the world were founded after 1993, and are all worth more than $500 billion.

Reference:(https://en.wikipedia.org/wiki/List_of_public_corporations_by_market_capitalization#Publicly_traded_companies)

856.

President Garfield's cause of death wasn't so much the bullet wound from his assassination attempt as much as it was the treatment he received afterward. His doctors' clumsy, unsanitary attempts to heal him resulted in a severe, painful infection that killed him three months later.

Reference: (https://www.pbs.org/newshour/health/dirty-painful-death-president-james-garfield)

857.

Cashews are not nuts or legumes, they are drupes. This funky sounding word actually just means "stone fruits" like peaches and plums.

Reference: (https://paleoflourish.com/are-cashews-nuts-legumes-drupes)

858.

In 2001, a seven foot bull shark bit off a boy's arm. His uncle not only saved the boy, but dived in after the shark, wrestled it to shore where the shark was shot, retrieved the boy's arm and it was sewn back on in the hospital.

Reference: (https://www.telegraph.co.uk/news/worldnews/northamerica/usa/1333379/Uncle-wrestles-shark-to-save-boys-severed-arm.html)

859.

Alaska doesn't have a rail connection to the rest of North America, and has to have its train shipped by barge.

Reference: (http://www.trainweb.org/ultradomes/features/bargeloading.html)

860.

"Predator" and "Die Hard" director John McTiernan served a federal prison sentence from 2013 to 2014 for perjury and wiretapping, during which he declared bankruptcy.

Reference: (https://en.wikipedia.org/wiki/John_McTiernan#Personal_life)

861.

The Night's Watch cloaks from "Game of Thrones" are made of $79 IKEA rugs.

Reference: (https://www.cnbc.com/2017/08/21/jon-snows-game-of-thrones-cloak-is-made-from-ikea-rugs.html)

862.

Youbou, a small town with a population of 966, has the last hand-set bowling alley in North America.

Reference: (https://en.wikipedia.org/wiki/Youbou,_British_Columbia)

863.

Nikki Cox of "Unhappily Ever After" fame appeared as a background dancer at 9 years old in the "Badder" Segment of Michael Jackson's Moonwalker.

Reference: (https://en.wikipedia.org/wiki/Moonwalker#"Badder")

864.

The Germans thought that the shotgun was too inhuman a weapon, and lodged a complaint against the U.S.

Reference: (https://owlcation.com/humanities/World-War-1-History-Germany-Declares-Shotgun-Inhumane)

865.

A scrapped Boeing 747 turned into a Californian wonder house. Permission from federal agencies was required as it looks like a plane crash from the air. The owner spent 15 years finding the ideal spot in the mountains. This required the parts to be helicoptered in.

Reference: (https://en.wikipedia.org/wiki/747_Wing_House)

866.

Zipf's Law states that in almost every language, the most common word will occur 2 times as often as the second most common word, 3 times as often as the third most common word, and so on.

Reference: (https://www.britannica.com/topic/Zipfs-law)

867.

In a review of clinical drug trials, almost all negative studies were unpublished, leading to the false impression that 93% of antidepressant trials had positive results. When unpublished studies were included, 51% of all clinical trials were positive and 49% were negative.

Reference: (https://www.ncbi.nlm.nih.gov/pmc/articles/PMC2580079/#R17)

868.

On March 7th, 1788, the Austrian army defeated itself. Believing they were under attack by Ottoman forces the Austrians fired on their own troops, ultimately leading to the deaths of 10,000 Austrian soldiers and the easy capture of Karansebes by the Ottoman Empire.

Reference: (https://www.worldatlas.com/articles/did-you-know-the-austrian-army-defeated-itself-in-the-1788-battle-of-karansebes.html)

869.

Lottie Williams is the only person to have been hit by re-entering space debris. She was walking through a park in Tulsa Oklahoma in January, 1997, at 3:30 AM and felt a tapping on her shoulder. It was a piece of the fuel tank of a Delta II rocket launched in 1996. She was unhurt.

Reference: (http://www.foxnews.com/tech/2011/09/21/woman-gets-hit-by-space-junk-lives-to-tell-tale.html)

870.

After a certain depth under water your lungs are compressed to a point where you are no longer buoyant and will sink to the bottom unless you have something to hold on to.

Reference: (https://youtu.be/0B0EhuxJsts?t=98)

871.

Fruity Pebbles cereal is just colored and flattened long-grain rice that is sprayed with a sugar and flavor mixture.

Reference: (https://www.foodnetwork.com/videos/fruity-pebbles-unwrapped-0156358)

872.

Jennifer Lawrence doused a fan in beer at a bar in Budapest after he told her off when she denied him a selfie.

Reference: (http://www.businessinsider.com/jennifer-lawrence-got-into-a-bar-fight-in-budapest-over-a-selfie-2017-9)

873.

For 36% of East Asians drinking alcohol, they will have facial flushing, nausea, tachycardia and a higher risk of esophageal cancer.

Reference: (https://www.ncbi.nlm.nih.gov/pmc/articles/PMC2659709)

874.

Beastie Boys, "Licensed to Ill" album made history in 1987 as the first rap album to hit number 1 on the Billboard 200 chart, and spent 7 straight weeks at number 1.

Reference: (https://www.billboard.com/articles/news/489107/beastie-boys-blazed-billboard-chart-history)

875.

Taco Bell first tried to enter the Mexican market in 1992, but its restaurants all closed within two years.

Reference: (https://www.fool.com/amp/investing/general/2013/11/09/5-things-you-probably-didnt-know-about-taco-bell.aspx)

876.

The set of Sesame Street was intentionally made to look like a poor inner city block, complete with trash and decay, because the original target audience was inner city children and the producers wanted it to feel familiar.

Reference: (https://en.wikipedia.org/wiki/History_of_Sesame_Street#Development)

877.

During a protest over the base jumping ban in Yellowstone National Park, a woman's shoot didn't open. She fell 3600 feet to her death in front of 150 spectators.

Reference: (https://www.sfgate.com/news/article/Parachutist-s-Death-Leaves-Her-Peers-With-Grief-2899709.php)

878.

In 1848, a traveling preacher was challenged to a duel by a "Desperado." As the challenged party, the preacher chose the weapons, it was potatoes.

Reference: (https://cdnc.ucr.edu/cgi-bin/cdnc?a=d&d=MJ18891128.2.6)

879.

The American forces in the Gulf of Tonkin incident, that sparked the Vietnam War, were commanded by Jim Morrison's dad.

Reference: (https://en.wikipedia.org/wiki/George_Stephen_Morrison)

880.

It it take minutes to strangle someone to death.

Reference: (https://en.wikipedia.org/wiki/Strangling)

881.

Of the 425,000 German prisoners of war in the United States, only 14 of them were executed. They were convicted of killing other prisoners for not being loyal to the Nazi cause. Many "suicides" were likely murders.

Reference: (https://en.wikipedia.org/wiki/German_prisoners_of_war_in_the_United_States)

882.

A disgruntled father irradiated his son from April to October, 1972, leading to sixteen surgeries and eventual castration.

Reference: (http://www.johnstonsarchive.net/nuclear/radevents/1972USA1.html)

883.

William Kamkwamba, at the age of 15, taught himself how to build windmills out of junk to provide his family electricity, and later to pump water for his community that was suffering from a huge drought. He did all of this through library books, as his family couldn't afford schooling.

Reference: (https://www.wired.com/2009/10/kamwamba-windmill/)

884.

There is a certain area of the face in which picking a pimple could lead to meningitis, amongst other brain-related disorders.

Reference: (http://www.freewebs.com/rogerqualo/CLINI/CavernousSinusThrombosis.htm)

885.

In 2012, a former Wall Street millionaire committed suicide by cyanide pill in court after receiving a guilty verdict for burning down his mansion in an elaborate tax fraud scheme.

Reference: (https://www.youtube.com/watch?v=fWO_O4ScAsg&feature=youtu.be)

886.

Abraham Lincoln's corpse was sent on a two-week funeral tour across America, shown openly to thousands. In the course of the trip the body visibly decomposed, bloated, and darkened. In New York City alone, the body was seen by over 150,000 and exposed to the air for 23 hours straight.

Reference:(http://www.slate.com/articles/life/history/2015/02/abraham_lincoln_s_decaying_corpse_was_sent_on_a_two_week_funeral_tour_across.html)

887.

Bone mineral, the inorganic component of bone and osseous tissue, has many names. One of them is "Bone Apatite".

Reference: (https://en.wikipedia.org/wiki/Bone_mineral)

888.

It has been alleged that the Chinese Doomsday Sect of "Eastern Lightning" abducted their targets for conversion and forced them to convert by employing beatings and coercive tactics.

Reference: (https://www.thedailybeast.com/is-this-the-scariest-doomsday-sect-in-china)

889.

The coco de mer, the world's largest seed, looks like a female buttocks and only grows on female Lodoicea trees, while male Lodoicea trees grow phallic flower clusters.

Reference: (https://en.wikipedia.org/wiki/Lodoicea)

890.

"The North Pond Hermit", or Christopher Thomas Knight, is a man who disappeared in the wilderness of Maine at the age of 20. He then proceeded to live the next 27 years in isolation surviving off of stolen goods from campsites before eventually being caught.

Reference: (https://www.gq.com/story/the-last-true-hermit)

891.

When the last person to be executed in Canada was told that he would most likely be the last one to be executed, he said "Some consolation."

Reference: (https://en.wikipedia.org/wiki/Arthur_Lucas)

892.

There is a North Korean propaganda film which is about their nuclear capabilities becoming so advanced that the U.S. president is forced to go to North Korea and accept them as a global super-power.

Reference: (https://www.38north.org/2012/08/jlewis083012/)

893.

The terms "left" and "right" appeared during the French Revolution of 1789 when members of the National Assembly divided into supporters of the king to the president's right and supporters of the revolution to his left.

Reference: (https://kpfa.org/player/?audio=280505)

894.

In World War II, the Brits intentionally reported on V2 Missiles hitting areas south of London, when in reality they were hitting London, so that the Nazis would think they were missing their target, thus correcting and sending the next V2s into less densely populated areas outside of London. It worked.

Reference: (https://en.wikipedia.org/wiki/V-2_rocket#Direct_attack)

895.

Even though Abraham Lincoln is known for the speech he gave, he was not the featured orator on the Gettysburg battlefield. Edward Everett, the featured orator, gave a 2 hour speech while Lincoln's speech was only about 2 minutes.

Reference: (https://mannerofspeaking.org/2010/11/19/the-gettysburg-address-an-analysis/)

896.

The wasabi we eat in the U.S. is fake. Real wasabi is hard to cultivate and expensive to mass produce.

Reference: (http://www.businessinsider.com/most-wasabi-served-in-the-us-is-fake-2017-1)

897.

"Mauvaise Foi", is a philosophical concept utilized to describe the phenomenon in which human beings, under pressure from social forces, adopt false values and disown their innate freedom, hence acting inauthentically.

Reference: (https://en.wikipedia.org/wiki/Bad_faith_(existentialism))

898.

Scientists found a dinosaur "mummy" with intact skin and armor.

Reference: (http://allthatsinteresting.com/nodosaur-dinosaur-mummy)

899.

China creates so much synthetic diamonds that are identical to real diamonds that prices of diamonds are being driven down. De Beers has created a university to study how to identify "natural" and "man-made" diamonds because no experts can tell the difference.

Reference: (http://www.scmp.com/business/companies/article/2076225/de-beers-fights-fakes-technology-chinas-lab-grown-diamonds)

900.

In 1956, in Tbilisi, Georgia, Soviet military troops suppressed mass demonstrations against Soviet leader Nikita Khrushchev's de-Stalinization policy.

Reference: (https://en.wikipedia.org/wiki/1956_Georgian_demonstrations)

901.

Taking over the counter anti-inflammatory medications like aspirin and ibuprofen may interfere with pregnancy.

Reference: (http://theconversation.com/what-marsupials-taught-us-about-embryo-implantation-could-help-women-using-ivf-81539)

902.

Honda created a "musical road" to play the William Tell Overture when driven over, but they forgot to take into account the width of the grooves when changing the spacing between them, so all the notes are wrong. Three years later the road was redone with the same mistake.

Reference: (http://davidsd.org/2008/12/honda-needs-a-tune-up/)

903.

Over 270 people were rescued in 2017 in the U.S. by using a beacon linked to SARSAT, a system used to locate mariners, aviators, and recreational enthusiasts in distress almost anywhere in the world at any time and in almost any condition.

Reference: (http://www.sarsat.noaa.gov/)

904.

Ugandan Derreck Kayongo collected barely-used hotel soaps that would otherwise get thrown out. He formed Global Soap Project, which recycles used soaps and distributes them free of charge to people who don't have access to basic sanitation.

Reference: (http://www.cnn.com/2011/US/06/16/cnnheroes.kayongo.hotel.soap/index.html)

905.

The Watkin's Tower in London was supposed to rival the Eiffel Tower, however, Gustave Eiffel refused to participate. After a contest for the design, it never went beyond the first stage which was tilting when it was destroyed. The legendary Wembley Stadium was built instead in 1923.

Reference:(https://en.wikipedia.org/wiki/Edward_Watkin#Wembley_Park_and_Watkin's_Tower
)

906.

Despite the fact that a majority of polls suggest the percentage of Americans who identify as Christians at 75%, about 90% of all Americans celebrate Christmas.

Reference: (https://www.washingtontimes.com/blog/watercooler/2013/dec/23/what-christmas-wars-90-percent-all-americans-celeb/)

907.

Aaron Hernandez's brain was shown, post-mortem, to have signs of CTE, a disease found in people who've suffered concussions or severe blows to the head. Symptoms include aggressiveness, explosiveness, impulsivity, depression, memory loss and other cognitive changes.

Reference: (https://en.wikipedia.org/wiki/Aaron_Hernandez#Death)

908.

Marilyn Monroe never intentionally posed for the first issue of Playboy. Hefner paid $500 to a Chicago calendar company for the photos which were taken 4 years earlier. Marilyn was paid $50 for the initial shoot and had to buy a copy of the magazine herself to see the photos.

Reference: (http://www.bbc.com/news/world-us-canada-41436975)

909.

The director of “My Cousin Vinny” has a law degree from Cambridge and the film is highly regarded in the legal community for its realistic depiction of courtroom procedure and trial strategy.

Reference: (https://en.wikipedia.org/wiki/My_Cousin_Vinny#Critical_reception)

910.

Iceland has the highest per-capita published books. 10% of the country's population will publish a book in their lifetimes.

Reference: (https://landlopers.com/2015/06/21/facts-about-iceland)

911.

CRISPR is an accurate gene editing tool that uses RNA to permanently modify genes in living cells and organisms. It is currently used to prevent mosquitoes from carrying plasmodia, the bacteria responsible for malaria. It is expected to have a profound impact during our lifetimes.

Reference: (https://www.broadinstitute.org/what-broad/areas-focus/project-spotlight/questions-and-answers-about-crispr)

912.

"Hot Tub Time Machine 2" was supposed to be named "Hot Tub Time Machine 3" as a play on the series premise, the characters would travel too far in time, but Paramount Studios thought that the title would be too confusing.

Reference: (https://www.cinemablend.com/new/Hot-Tub-Time-Machine-2-Had-Hysterical-Title-Until-Studio-Changed-It-69877.html)

913.

Journalist Annie Jacobsen claims the USSR operated on children to make them look like extra-terrestrials, then put them in a saucer like craft and dropped them over the United States as part of a plan to cause panic within the U.S. government.

Reference: (https://www.npr.org/2011/05/17/136356848/area-51-uncensored-was-it-ufos-or-the-ussr)

914.

A 2010 study found Ozzy Osbourne to carry several hundred thousand genome variants that have never been seen by scientists, which make him less susceptible to the harms of drugs and alcohol.

Reference: (https://www.theguardian.com/music/2010/nov/05/ozzy-osbourne-genes-sequenced-genome)

915.

The 9/11 attacks played a large part in the downfall of the Concorde supersonic aircraft because many of the consistent New York City to London passengers worked in the Twin Towers.

Reference: (https://www.heritageconcorde.com/concorde-and-the-twin-towers-attack)

916.

The University of Louisiana-Monroe has won 28 out of 39 possible national water ski championships, their longest streak being 1980 to 1990, and 14 out of the last 18 years.

Reference: (http://www.usawaterski.org/pages/divisions/collegiate/main.asp)

917.

When Mount Pelée erupted in 1902, the blast killed all but one of St. Pierre's thirty thousand citizens. He only survived because he was underground, having been thrown into a dungeon for starting a bar fight.

Reference: (https://www.theguardian.com/world/2002/apr/28/physicalsciences.highereducation)

918.

The human body is surrounded by clouds of skin and fart bacteria.

Reference: (https://www.wired.com/2015/09/body-surrounded-clouds-skin-fart-bacteria)

919.

Hands-On Gene Editing is now a middle school class.

Reference: (https://www.npr.org/sections/alltechconsidered/2017/05/27/530210657/how-a-gene-editing-tool-went-from-labs-to-a-middle-school-classroom)

920.

Before he became an actor, Phil Hartman designed album covers for bands such as Poco and America.

Reference: (https://en.wikipedia.org/wiki/Phil_Hartman)

921.

The United Kingdom has a silly season, also known as Cucumber Time, which is punctuated by a larger than average amount of frivolous news stories.

Reference: (https://en.wikipedia.org/wiki/Silly_season)

922.

Howard Mwikuta was the first player born and raised in Africa to appear in the NFL when he played for the Dallas Cowboys in the 1970 pre-season as a placekicker.

Reference: (https://en.wikipedia.org/wiki/Howard_Mwikuta)

923.

California does not allow you to name your child using anything other than the 26 English letters. Meaning that José is a banned name in California.

Reference:(https://en.wikipedia.org/wiki/Naming_in_the_United_States#Names_with_accents_and/or_non-English_letters)

924.

The first film made in Hollywood was “In Old California” and it was just 17 minutes long. For years, everyone thought the first film was “The Squaw Man” but that was just the first feature film.

Reference: (https://en.wikipedia.org/wiki/In_Old_California_(1910_film))

925.

Chicago Blackhawks Genera Manager Stan Bowman is named after the Stanley Cup. Bowman's father, legendary coach Scotty Bowman, won his first Stanley Cup a month before Stan's birth.

Reference: (https://en.wikipedia.org/wiki/Stan_Bowman#Personal_Life)

926.

A Bahraini princess Meriam Al-Khalifa eloped with a U.S. Marine, was nearly assassinated for it, didn't like her reduced lifestyle, divorced in Las Vegas and went back to Bahrain.

Reference: (https://en.wikipedia.org/wiki/Meriam_Al_Khalifa)

927.

Qatar is building a 40,000 seat stadium out of shipping containers that can be quickly disassembled and reassembled at a new location.

Reference: (https://www.curbed.com/2017/11/29/16714408/shipping-container-architecture-qatar-world-cup-stadium-2022)

928.

Toilet wine is fermented fruit juice made from moldy bread, oranges, a ton of sugar; kept warm in showers with convicts; and then strained through a used sock.

Reference: (http://www.lamag.com/drinkrecipes/how-to-make-prison-wine-the-craft-version/)

929.

The famous instrumental theme song to the James Bond film "On Her Majesty's Secret Service" lack lyrics because composer John Barry thought any lyrics would have to written in the style of Gilbert and Sullivan.

Reference: (https://en.wikipedia.org/wiki/On_Her_Majesty%27s_Secret_Service_(soundtrack))

930.

In 1965, a Welsh village was flooded as a result of a private bill sponsored by the Liverpool City Council to make a reservoir, which was approved in Parliament. Consequently, the Liverpool Council did not need permission from the Welsh authorities and the inhabitant's houses were submerged.

Reference: (https://www.liverpoolecho.co.uk/news/liverpool-news/incredible-pictures-show-welsh-village-10284365)

931.

King George III has been posthumously diagnosed with Porphyria, causing his urine to turn blue. His doctors gave him medicine contaminated with arsenic, worsening his condition.

Reference: (https://io9.gizmodo.com/the-king-who-peed-blue-930843334)

932.

The deadline for the coming of the Jewish Messiah is only 222 years away.

Reference: (https://en.wikipedia.org/wiki/Year_6000)

933.

A woman in Florida married a Ferris Wheel that she named Bruce.

Reference: (https://www.huffingtonpost.com/2013/11/18/linda-ducharme_n_4298963.html)

934.

There are 14 names listed on the Vietnam Wall memorial who are not actually deceased but were included nonetheless do to clerical error. Their names have not been removed, but if a panel ever needs to be replaced then the plan is for the incorrect names to be removed at that time.

Reference: (http://www.nytimes.com/1991/02/11/us/on-memorial-to-the-dead-14-who-live.html)

935.

Aztec midwifes advised women to continue having sex until the 7th month of pregnancy, saying that, if women abstained, their children would be sickly and weak.

Reference: (https://www.nationalgeographic.com/archaeology-and-history/magazine/2017/01-02/aztec-midwife-practical-pregnancy-care/)

936.

In 1990, Sinéad O'Connor refused to give a concert in New Jersey, because the organizers insisted on playing the American National Anthem before her act. Frank Sinatra then threatened to “kick her in the ass” and New Jersey prohibited her from ever singing in that concert hall again.

Reference: (http://articles.latimes.com/1990-08-28/entertainment/ca-409_1_national-anthem)

937.

Astronauts exercise 2.5 hours a day to keep their bodies from atrophying in zero gravity.

Reference: (https://www.youtube.com/watch?v=xnCdDtcB6GM)

938.

In 1824, the crew of a ship killed the captain and officers, and each other, then pacific islanders killed most of the remaining crew. Two of the survivors lived with the natives until rescued two years later.

Reference: (http://www.gutenberg.org/files/28955/28955-h/28955-h.htm)

939.

May 4th is unofficially celebrated as Dave Brubeck day because 5/4 represents the time signature of "Take Five," arguably Brubeck's most well-known song.

Reference: (https://en.wikipedia.org/wiki/Dave_Brubeck)

940.

The most valuable dollhouse in the world, Automat Castle, is worth 8.5 million dollars and contains original works of art, gold chandeliers, inlaid marble bathrooms, artifacts from Pompeii, and the world's smallest antique Bible.

Reference: (https://en.wikipedia.org/wiki/Astolat_Dollhouse_Castle)

941.

In 2002, Microsoft forgot to pay to renew one of their domains and a random guy paid the bill so he could check his Hotmail.

Reference: (https://www.cnet.com/news/good-samaritan-squashes-hotmail-lapse/)

942.

Giant tortoises on whaling voyages were stored helplessly on their backs for up to six months before being killed and eaten. While alive, they drank gallons of water at a time and kept it in a special bladder, making a properly-butchered tortoise a source of cool, perfectly drinkable water.

Reference: (http://qi.com/infocloud/giant-tortoises)

943.

Kosmos 954 is a nuclear powered Soviet satellite. In 1978, it burned up on reentry to the atmosphere, scattering radioactive debris across northern Canada, and prompting an extensive cleanup operation known as Operation Morning Light.

Reference: (https://en.wikipedia.org/wiki/Kosmos_954)

944.

King Neptune, a pig that was a U.S. Navy mascot between 1942 and 1946, helped raise 19 million in war bonds to build the USS Illinois.

Reference: (https://en.wikipedia.org/wiki/King_Neptune_(pig))

945.

Most European countries don't collect information on race and ethnicity in their census.

Reference: (https://en.wikipedia.org/wiki/Race_and_ethnicity_in_censuses)

946.

Thaddeus Stevens was a US Congress member who was fiercely anti-slavery and anti-racist. He pushed for the confiscation of land from white planters to be distributed to the freedmen during Reconstruction. Deemed too radical, his proposal was rejected.

Reference: (https://en.wikipedia.org/wiki/Thaddeus_Stevens)

947.

The Altamont Free Concert was a rock concert known for its considerable violence, including three accidental deaths and the stabbing death of a man by the Hells Angels, who had been contracted to serve as a security guard at the event.

Reference: (https://en.wikipedia.org/wiki/Altamont_Free_Concert)

948.

Giraffe bread is the exact same thing as Tiger bread. Sainsbury's renamed it to Giraffe bread after receiving a letter from a 3 year old girl saying it looked more like giraffe.

Reference: (http://www.bbc.co.uk/news/business-16812545)

949.

The director of "Ace Ventura," Tom Shadyac sustained a brain injury from a bicycle accident causing serious depression. His recovery inspired him to film the documentary, "I Am", about human connectedness, and to abandon his materialistic lifestyle.

Reference: (https://en.wikipedia.org/wiki/Tom_Shadyac)

950.

Boston Red Sox Out Fielder Mookie Betts bowled a perfect 300 at the World Series of Bowling, in the same week he was awarded an MLB Gold Glove.

Reference: (https://www.si.com/mlb/2017/11/13/red-sox-mookie-betts-bowls-300)

951.

Blue Cat Blues is the final episode of "Tom and Jerry" ending with both committing suicide.

Reference: (https://en.wikipedia.org/wiki/Blue_Cat_Blues)

952.

After World War II, 250,000 tons of Nazi bombs containing nerve agents were left outside on a runway in Wales until they corroded and leaked. They were subsequently carefully repaired before being dumped in the Irish Sea a few years later.

Reference: (https://en.wikipedia.org/wiki/Operation_Sandcastle)

953.

Elmer's Glue has a serving size.

Reference: (http://www.myfitnesspal.com/food/calories/elmers-school-glue-379264070)

954.

Palau announced it would create the world's first shark sanctuary banning commercial shark fishing. The sanctuary protects about 230,000 square miles of ocean. Palau received the Future Policy Award from World Future Council, because, "Palau is a global leader in protecting marine ecosystems."

Reference: (https://en.wikipedia.org/wiki/Palau#Sanctuary)

955.

Thousands of fishermen die every year on Lake Victoria during intense night-time thunderstorms.

Reference: (https://www.ncbi.nlm.nih.gov/pmc/articles/PMC5036145/)

956.

In December 2013, Tinder had its first Antarctica match between an American McMurdo Station scientist and visiting camper, a 45 minute helicopter ride away.

Reference: (https://www.thecut.com/2014/02/tinder-makes-its-first-match-in-antarctica.html)

957.

McDonalds had an unsuccessful burger released in Norway called the McAfrica in 2002.

Reference: (https://money.howstuffworks.com/5-failed-mcdonalds-menu-items5.htm)

958.

In Hawaii during World War II, very few Japanese-Americans were sent to Internment Camps after the bombing of Pearl Harbor. This was due to the fact they were so vital to Hawaii's economy.

Reference: (https://www.nbcnews.com/news/asian-america/untold-story-japanese-americans-wwii-internment-hawaii-n170746)

959.

The Florida senator, Bill Nelson, was an astronaut on the Space Shuttle mission STS-61-C.

Reference: (https://en.wikipedia.org/wiki/STS-61-C)

960.

Regular physical activity increases total blood volume which in turn assists with heat dissipation, body temperature stability, reducing strokes, and improving cardiovascular stability. The opposite is true when blood volume is decreased during periods of physical inactivity.

Reference: (https://www.ncbi.nlm.nih.gov/pubmed/17630597/)

961.

Tom Selleck's first film role was a bit role, credited as "Stud" in the film adaptation of Gore Vidal's "Myra Breckenridge," after starring in Pepsi commercials in the late 1960s.

Reference: (https://en.wikipedia.org/wiki/Tom_Selleck#Early_work_and_Magnum,_P.I.)

962.

Ludwigshafen in Germany produced much of the poison gas used during the First World War. It was the first city ever strategically bombed from the air when the French attacked its chemical plants.

Reference: (https://en.wikipedia.org/wiki/Ludwigshafen)

963.

A Japanese World War II soldier held out for 30 years in the Philippines jungle, refusing to believe the war had ended.

Reference: (http://www.realclearlife.com/history/hiroo-onoda-fought-wwii-for-30-years-too-long/)

964.

Sailors aboard submarines work 6 hour shifts so that it is easier for them to give their undivided attention to the equipment they operate during a shorter shift. The military also switched submarines from an 18-hour work day to a traditional 24-hour one, improving morale significantly.

Reference: (https://www.military.com/daily-news/2015/10/16/submarine-force-now-24hour-work-day.html)

965.

In his later years, Rembrandt drew paintings of Mughal miniatures known as "Suratse tekeningen".

Reference: (http://www.thehindu.com/entertainment/art/rembrandts-mughal-era/article22918160.ece/amp/)

966.

In 1798, Congress passed the Alien and Sedition Acts, which prohibited newspapers from publishing, "false, scandalous, or malicious writing", against the government, including any public opposition to any law or presidential act. This act was in effect until 1801.

Reference: (https://en.wikipedia.org/wiki/Media_bias#History)

967.

10% of all bombs dropped on London in World War II didn't detonate, and are still regularly found to this day.

Reference: (http://www.bbc.com/future/story/20150922-these-nazi-bombs-are-more-dangerous-now-than-ever-before)

968.

Logging, fishing, and aircraft piloting are the top 3 most dangerous jobs in America, while law enforcement and firefighting are ranked 15th on the list. Taxi drivers are more than twice as likely to be murdered on the job as law enforcement personnel.

Reference: (https://www.cbsnews.com/pictures/the-20-deadliest-jobs-in-america-ranked/)

969.

In 1997, you could meet a women who met Vincent Van Gogh when she was a child.

Reference: (https://en.wikipedia.org/wiki/Oldest_people)

970.

Tom Fogerty, rhythm guitarist of Creedence Clearwater Revival and brother of John Fogerty, contracted HIV from an unscreened blood transfusion following back surgery in the 1980s and died of HIV complicated tuberculosis in 1990.

Reference: (https://en.wikipedia.org/wiki/Tom_Fogerty#Death)

971.

Modern dog breed classification started with the Victorians, in England, in the 19th century.

Reference: (https://en.wikipedia.org/wiki/Dog_breed#History)

972.

Kobe Bryant grew up in Italy, and can speak fluent Italian.

Reference: (https://www.youtube.com/watch?v=kwkMf6R3qSA)

973.

U.S. forces bombarded North Korea so thoroughly during the Korean War that by the end of the war, crews had to jettison their payload at sea because they had run out of things to bomb.

Reference: (https://en.wikipedia.org/wiki/Bombing_of_North_Korea_1950-1953)

974.

Formula 1 World Champion Kimi Raikkonen, nicknamed "The Ice Man", was so calm before his debut race in 2001 that he was asleep 30 minutes before the start.

Reference: (https://en.wikipedia.org/wiki/Kimi_R%C3%A4ikk%C3%B6nen#Sauber_(2001))

975.

Your brain is able to make a decision for you seconds before you become aware of the fact that you are making a decision
Reference: (https://www.nature.com/news/2008/080411/full/news.2008.751.html)

976.

Costa Rica surpassed the U.S. in life expectancy in the late 1980s.

Reference: (https://www.theguardian.com/working-in-development/2017/oct/07/how-to-avert-the-apocalypse-take-lessons-from-costa-rica)

977.

There was a player for the Los Angeles Lakers, AC Green, who maintained his virginity throughout his entire 16 year NBA career.

Reference: (https://uproxx.com/movies/adam-mckay-interview-basketball-ac-green/)

978.

Piasecki Aircraft designed and built an unmanned quadcopter in 1958.

Reference: (http://www.piasecki.com/piaseckifirsts.php)

979.

Owls have been observed bringing Texas Blind Snakes to their nest, where the will eat the parasites that affect the owl chicks.

Reference: (https://en.wikipedia.org/wiki/Leptotyphlops_dulcis#Diet)

980.

During the development cycle of Super Smash Bros. Melee on the GameCube, director Masahiro Sakurai worked for 13 months straight without a single rest day. On some occasions, Sakurai would work for nearly two days straight with just a four hour nap at home.

Reference:(http://www.nintendolife.com/news/2014/10/sounds_like_super_smash_bros_director_masahiro_sakurai_sure_could_use_a_break)

981.

The 15th century Islamic mosaics in Spain's Alhambra palace display a near-perfect understanding of mathematical logic and 16 of 17 types of symmetry identified by modern mathematicians.

Reference: (http://observer.com/2017/04/did-artists-lead-the-way-in-mathematics-fraud-patterns-geometry-history/)

982.

Even the farthest star with mass in the universe have a gravitational effect on us.

Reference: (https://en.wikipedia.org/wiki/Gravity)

983.

Popular singer James Blunt was a military captain and a champion skier.

Reference: (https://en.wikipedia.org/wiki/James_Blunt)

984.

The insult, “a wimp”, comes from Popeye the Sailor.

Reference: (https://www.telegraph.co.uk/books/childrens-books/popeye-10-things-you-never-knew/)

985.

In 1982, Delta employees banded together and accepted $30 million in payroll deductions to purchase the first Boeing 767 for the company.

Reference: (http://www.airlinereporter.com/2010/10/the-spirit-of-delta-air-lines-the-gift-of-a-boeing-767/)

986.

The U.S. planned to put thousands of small "kill vehicles" in orbit to destroy Soviet ICBMs. This system, known as Brilliant Pebbles, became the chief focus of Reagan's "Star Wars" program.

Reference: (https://en.wikipedia.org/wiki/Brilliant_Pebbles)

987.

The antipode of any spot on Earth is the point on Earth's surface diametrically opposite to it. Approximately 15% of land is antipodal to other land.

Reference: (https://en.wikipedia.org/wiki/Antipodes)

988.

Until it was surpassed by "It" 18 years later in 2017, "The Sixth Sense" was the highest-grossing horror film of all time.

Reference: (https://en.wikipedia.org/wiki/The_Sixth_Sense)

989.

The crew of the EP-3 ARIES II involved in the Hainan Island incident of 2001 resorted to pouring hot coffee over sensitive material in the plane, as they were not trained on how to properly destroy sensitive documents and equipment.

Reference: (https://en.wikipedia.org/wiki/Hainan_Island_incident)

990.

Before 1917, the British royal family had no last name at all simply because they were so famous they didn't need one.

Reference: (https://www.independent.co.uk/life-style/british-royal-family-surname-last-name-a7519901.html)

991.

It is illegal to name your child "Brfxxccxxmnpcccclllmmnprxvclmnckssqlbb1116" in Sweden.

Reference:(https://en.wikipedia.org/wiki/Naming_law_in_Sweden#Brfxxccxxmnpcccclllmmnprxvclmnckssqlbb11116)

992.

There are nerve endings that exist only to recognize a gentle stroking touch. Their activation decreases the heart rate and activates the smile muscle. Their optimal speed is 3 to 5 centimeters per second, which means we are genetically wired to cuddle and caress each other at predetermined velocities.

Reference: (http://journals.plos.org/plosone/article?id=10.1371/journal.pone.0173457)

993.

During the SARS epidemic in 2004, a 45-year-old Taiwanese woman died from alcohol poisoning after immersing herself in a bathtub full of 40% alcohol for 12 hours, likely because she thought the alcohol would decontaminate her if she had been exposed to the virus.

Reference: (http://unusualdeaths.com/category/taiwan/)

994.

Earthworms are not native to the American great lakes region.

Reference: (http://msue.anr.msu.edu/news/the_dirt_about_earthworms)

995.

In rural Kyrgyzstan, men still marry their women the old-fashioned way, by abducting them off the street and forcing them to be their wife.

Reference: (https://www.youtube.com/watch?v=DKAusMNTNnk)

996.

Doritos originated as a way for the Disneyland restaurant "Casa de Fritos" to recycle stale tortillas instead of throwing them away.

Reference: (https://gizmodo.com/how-doritos-went-from-disneyland-dumpster-to-multi-bill-1571523236/amp)

997.

There are open captions as well as closed captions. Open captions are part of the video and cannot be turned on and off.

Reference: (https://www.washington.edu/accessit/print.html?ID=1050)

998.

Charlize Theron's father was shot and killed by her mother.

Reference: (https://www.huffingtonpost.com/2012/10/04/charlize-therons-childhood-home-scene-grisly-murder_n_1939111.html)

999.

The Zika virus might be a possible cure for cancer.

Reference: (https://www.sciencenewsforstudents.org/article/could-zika-become-cancer-treatment)

1000.

Holidays in Scotland are all over the map. For example, "Spring Holiday" is observed in some cities on the first Monday in April; some on the second Monday; Edinburgh on the third Monday; one town on the last Monday; and Aberdeen switches it up from year to year.

Reference: (https://en.wikipedia.org/wiki/Public_and_bank_holidays_in_Scotland)

Printed in Great
Britain
by Amazon

31084007R00092